The Mulberry Juice Dress

To Lisa

Maggie Kranshaar

The Mulberry Juice Dress

and other tales of Lebanon

Margaret Freidinger Kraushaar

FITHIAN PRESS • SANTA BARBARA • 1996

Published by Fithian Press
A division of Daniel and Daniel, Publishers, Inc.
Post Office Box 1525
Santa Barbara, CA 93102

Design by Karim Marouf

Kraushaar, Margaret Freidinger, date
        The mulberry juice dress, and other stories of Lebanon / Margaret
    Freidinger Kraushaar.
                p.   cm.
        ISBN 1-56474-176-1 (pbk. : alk. paper)
        1. Kraushaar, Margaret Freidinger, date.   2. Children of missionaries —
    Lebanon — Biography. I. Title.
    BV2094.5.K73 1996
    956.92'035'092 - dc20
    [B]   96-5261
                                                            CIP

To Thalassa

• Table of Contents •

Acknowledgements

These stories are all true, though some are more true than others—embroidered, my mother would have said. The truth here is, after all, my truth, and we each make our own.

I am aware that some of the "stories," especially the last three, are essays and journal entries rather than stories, and that they differ in tone from the earlier ones. I considered leaving them out, but I included them finally; they emerged so naturally after the earlier ones that there was no way I could do that.

I want to acknowledge by name:

Anne Byerly Moore, my cherished friend and roommate at American Community School, who generously offered to put my manuscript in shape and has made sense out of my Arabic transliterations;

Lenore Coberly, writer and teacher in Madison, Wisconsin, who persuaded me that the first assignment I did for her was not a short story, but a packed ball of many stories that I must unravel, patiently and unhurriedly, to allow each one its space;

Karen Updike, Madison poet and teacher, who understood what I was trying to say, sometimes before I did;

My children, Mark, Sunna, and Andy, daughters-in-law Jackie and Dianne, who all encouraged me along the way (though Mark, a poet, scourged me for using too many words);

My brother Art, with whom I live, my brother Philip and his family, my sister Anne (Anna), my cousin Andy March;

My dear friends, Lucie Hangstefer, Jan Watson, Pat and Jim Sterling (Jim who kept saying, "Send it to *The New Yorker!* "), Laura Smail, Jean Duesler, Don Cox and Ellen Reicher, Mary Louise Symon.

10 •

Also, thank you, members of my writing groups on Whidbey Island here in Washington, for listening and urging me on, week after week.

I have changed the names of friends and schoolmates to allow them anonymity.

Seattle, Washington
January 1994

• Part One •

Going Back

Spring in our garden in Souk-el-Gharb displayed nine tall chinaberry trees with their frail sprays of purple flowers. We called them by their Arab name, zinzilacht. Outside the village the terraced hills grew green with new spring wheat. Melting snow crept down the mountains and oozed underfoot. Pale pink cyclamen and anemones with their hairy stems and purplish blue heads poked up between the stones.

Summer brought sirocco, breathless heat of dry wind and dust that turned mud roads to powder and grayed the mulberry trees on either side. When the wheat was gathered in, men threshed and winnowed it, filling the air with chaff. No rain fell all summer; hardly a cloud crossed the sky. Brilliant, unrelenting sunlight saturated our world until, with scarcely a warning twilight, nightfall and quick coolness. The sea, all bright and glimmering by day, dimmed, the horizon blurred. Ships' lights looked like drowning stars.

On summer nights the garden was loud with crickets. Zinzilacht trees, immense and heavy with leaves, rustled to each other. My brothers shook the trees and got a shower of green berries, hard as marbles, for their slingshots. Outside the village from the terraced vineyards came the sweet, warm smell of figs, bursting ripe.

Then gradually, gradually, a change: leaves dropped, nights grew cold, filled with shooting stars, and the rains and winds came. Snow spread downward on the Lebanon. In the garden, the bare zinzilachts let go the last of their fruit, yellow and mushy, to the ground. Frost edged the grass; the first ice slicked the pond.

Winter: short days and long nights, a time for gathering around the black iron stove, for eating lentil soup ladled out of the white tureen, for my mother to knit, for me to read aloud, and for our cook to tell us stories, while we waited for spring.

13

Tea in the garden, Zahleh, 1925

•

Our plane dove steeply and fast, like a kingfisher, to the Beirut airport. This was the summer of 1970, when only the leisured rich could afford to come by steamer anymore. I missed that more measured and ceremonial way to return, the way we had in 1931 after a furlough year in the United States.

I remembered walking down the gangplank into the waiting arms of Grandpa and Grandma, my mother's parents, missionaries like us. Retired now, they'd chosen to stay on in Lebanon instead of going back to New England. Grandpa was small and springy, with a black beard and black eyes. Mother looked like him; but the person who looked most like him was Haile Selassie. When the newsreels began showing pictures of the Lion of Judah, Emperor of Abyssinia, I thought he must be Grandpa dressed up. Grandma was small, too, with fine, pale hair she rolled into a sausage on top of her head. In front of the roll, she wore a flat velvet bow to cover her thinning place, with a matching piece of velvet at her neck.

After we kissed and hugged Grandpa and Grandma, him through his lovely beard, her through the scent of verbena, we could see who else had come down to the dock: the other mission people and school friends and whole families of Lebanese neighbors from Souk-el-Gharb, our hill village above Beirut. The grownups exclaimed over how much we had grown, and our neighbors asked in Arabic if we still remembered how to speak it after a whole year away. The girls "oohed" over how American my dress and shoes and even my socks looked, and we hugged and kissed. That is, my sister and I and our mother did, not my father or my two older brothers. We children learned early the confusing rules of kissing and hugging, ours and the Lebanese. Lebanese men kissed and hugged each other but not my father or brothers. Lebanese men kissed their mothers and children but not their wives. Lebanese women hugged and kissed other women and all children, even us.

Now, thirty-three years later, I got off the plane with my husband and two of my teenage children, and this time no one met us. My head was prepared for this, but not my heart. My grandparents had died in Lebanon before we left, my parents, one following the other, after they retired in the States. No one would meet us, or even expect us. Since my parents' deaths, I had lost track of the Lebanese families in Souk-el-Gharb, and I never had known their family names, only first names like Lulu, Aziz, Khalil, or Im Jurius (mother of Jurius), Abou Butrous (father of Butrous), or Ibn Ilyes (son of Ilyes).

Through the steamy airport building moved a sea of people dressed in mixed Arab and occidental clothes. I heard Arabic—men's loud shouting mostly—but couldn't understand much. Our family had learned to speak colloquial Lebanese Arabic; Syrians, Egyptians, Saudis, and Palestinians each spoke a different Arabic. Besides, my Arabic vocabulary, what I remembered of it, was that of a nine-year-old, my age when I began boarding school in Beirut. At fifteen, in 1937, I had gone away to the States with my parents and younger sister. This was my first return.

The airport seemed like an enormous marketplace, confusing yet familiar, until I noticed the khaki uniformed men—army apparently, rather than police—standing with legs apart, guns in front of their chests, at the entrances and exits. They looked unreal, like something on the six o'clock news, but menacing nonetheless, and nothing like the French *gendarmerie* I remembered in navy blue, piped with red, with natty visored caps. I had thought them very handsome and I liked to stare at them, especially if they stared back and winked at me. The Lebanese police had been like friendly uncles. One of them might stop my father for speeding, then chat and wave him on.

These men in the airport were a different species. I felt the tension around them and saw them as totally out of place in the Lebanon I knew. A year later the war began, but at the time I was only aware of finally coming home and of wanting nothing to get in the way of that.

At the exit doors taxi drivers rushed up offering to take us to the St. George, the Hilton or any other fancy hotel where

Grandma and Grandpa March

foreign tourists went. I said in Arabic that we needed a chauffeur to take us to Melcone's *pension* in Shemlan, a neighboring village to Souk.

The drivers understood what I said and were full of flattery about my accent—they would guess me to be a *bint Arab*, daughter of the Arabs. My husband and children had heard me speak Arabic now and then, short set pieces, proving I could; this dialogue with several taxi drivers at once was the real thing, not a parlor trick. The drivers shoved each other, vying to be chosen. I picked an older, solid-looking man who introduced himself as Nikola. I dickered with him about the cost, a heady experience, except that I had no idea what he should charge or how to translate the pounds and piasters he named. We paid double what we should have, but I didn't find that out till later.

The drive wasn't as exciting as it used to be. The hairpin turns had been engineered out, and Nikola's driving was majestic, while my father's had been impatient and fast, sometimes vengeful. To liven things up, my children showed off their Arabic (some indecent swear words I'd taught them and forgotten about). Nikola complimented them but gave me a look of reprimand, as though I were his wayward daughter who had corrupted his grandchildren.

When we used to travel the long road home from boarding school, we had the feeling we were journeying to another world. The trip was considered too long for us to go home between vacations. Now it took half an hour. Nikola told me that now many people commuted from work in Beirut to their homes in Souk-el-Gharb or Shemlan.

We came to Souk first. On the outskirts I asked Nikola to drive slowly. He smiled and we proceeded, as though in a hearse, down the one street, three blocks long. First came the hotel on the right, a two-story stone building with its name in neon script, "The New Farouk." The hotel used to have the only telephone in town, but its gambling casino made it forbidden territory except in emergencies. I remember how it lured me with its mystery and sophistication. I felt an echo of the same lure.

Main Street, Souk-el-Gharb

The butcher shop next door used to display whole sheep and quarters of beef hanging from hooks in the ceiling. I would dawdle by, held and horrified by the tubs of fresh, bloody entrails under clouds of flies. Village dogs always sniffed around the doorway. There was still a butcher shop, but no meat open to the air, no tubs of entrails, so no flies and no dogs. I missed them.

The shop next door still sold rice, chickpeas, and *burghul* from burlap bags on the floor. I glimpsed the great brass scales I remembered hanging near the door.

The cloth shop next to it had expanded behind glass front windows, so the bolts of cloth no longer seemed to flow out into the street. I remembered the special smell of new cloth and how it mixed in with my excitement about having a new dress made.

Down a way, and still the busiest spot in the village, was the coffeehouse where the men went to drink, play backgammon, and smoke the *nargili* (water pipe) when it came around.

Across the street the public oven looked deserted. There, our cook and other women of the village would bring their raw loaves of bread to be baked. This was afternoon. Maybe all the baking was done for the day.

A little farther along was the public fountain. It used to be a busy spot, where the women talked as they rested with their water jars between trips. No one was there now.

Souk-el-Gharb was a Christian village, so there was no mosque or *muezzin*'s tower. Up the hill on the left was the Greek Orthodox church, and a little farther the Maronite church. Down a side street to the right there used to be a small Protestant church where my mother played the organ. If my father was not examining native schools or arbitrating differences among church members in other villages so that he had to be away ("on tour" he called it), he would sometimes fill in for the regular Lebanese minister. Whichever one of them preached, the sermon would be in high Arabic, and it was a long hour. I wanted to ask Nikola to turn down the road to the church, but I remembered it wouldn't be open. We would have to go on Sunday.

Each church had its own bell sound, the heaviest and most sonorous being the Greek Orthodox. When someone of that faith died, the church bell tolled the age of the deceased, and everyone knew most solemnly who it was. I told my husband and children about the bells, wishing they could hear them now.

After thinking about it all these years, I longed to see my house. I knew I could find it blindfolded. But I stopped myself, to hold the savor for the next day. Nikola turned at the fountain and drove us on to Shemlan.

The next morning we walked to Souk-el-Gharb. Terraces still followed the contours of the hills as they used to, interrupted at intervals by villages whose names I no longer knew. Below us, closer than I expected, lay Beirut and the sand beaches I remembered as a child when we swam in that warm sea. I picked a sprig of wild thyme and held it to my nose. I thought how often I'd walked this road with my family or my friends, seldom alone. Suddenly I remembered a time when I'd walked it alone. I was twelve, coming home after an Arabic lesson. It was dark by the time I got home. The minute I walked in my father came at me in a rage. "Why are you so late? What were you doing after your lesson? Tell me the truth. What happened?"

I couldn't think what I had done to make him so angry.

Then he said, "Don't you know how dangerous it is for a young girl to walk alone at night between the Druse villages?"

The Druse were a special kind of Moslem, secretive in their beliefs and ways. Druse men could know the mysteries of their faith, the women not. Only the men attended religious services. I thought of the Druse men I had seen as having something ominous hidden on them, like a dagger tucked away, but in fact I'd never known any Druse men. At that moment, though, I responded not so much to "Druse" as to the words "young girl." I thought of myself as a child; my mother referred to my sister and me as "the little girls." Hearing my father call me a "young girl" and hearing the fear in his voice, I was flattered and frightened at the same time.

My father said, "You know a Druse was killed this past week in Aineb. Do you know what could happen now?"

I had heard it said that if anyone killed a Druse, the dead man's village would seek out and kill two Christians in retribution.

My father calmed himself down, seeing that I was safe. He even realized I had not intentionally frightened him and my mother. As a child, I treated the cautionary rules of adults with scorn, but I recognized belatedly that my father's fears were valid, his reaction understandable.

Now, all these years later, I had lost track of time and thought we must be halfway to Souk, but suddenly, there we were. Turn right at the fountain, go up and around the curve, walk a little farther, and there was our gate in our wall.

At first glance the house looked unchanged, though I saw at once that the garden was a wilderness. The summer house had disappeared, along with the fish pond and stone walks. I had a picture of my father scooping up pails of water from the pond and staggering with them, slopping, down the stone walks to his dahlias. But of course there were no dahlias, no *zinzilacht* trees. Then I noticed the iron grills were out of their windows, leaning against the walls. Half the shutters were gone.

A young woman came out of the house and asked us, unsmiling, what we wanted. Now that I was back in the land of my childhood, and standing at my childhood door, I expected—like a child—to be welcomed. I explained that I had grown up in this house. Still no smile but yes, we could come in. We went in awkwardly, feeling like intruders.

I thought to see our old parlor, enormous, whitewashed, with pillars and arches down the middle. Instead there were three rooms that made up the woman's apartment. The stone floors were gone, covered by gray linoleum. In summer, those floors had been smooth and cool under our bare feet. I could feel them still. On cleaning day the thin oriental scatter rugs were taken up and slung over lines in the garden to be beaten, and then the floors were sloshed with water and swept. Now the smell of wet stone came back to me, along with the smell of lemon we used with pumice to polish the brass trays and bowls.

The woman offered us chairs, and we sat down. She didn't sit down with us. Instead, I heard her at the door calling to a child and telling him in Arabic to run to the shop in the village to tell her husband that foreigners had shown up at their door. He was to come home to take care of the matter.

I sat remembering this house, glad not to talk. I thought of how it used to feel in winter. Its high ceilings and stone floors took on a damp chill that stayed all winter long. But there were warm places in the house: the dining room where we ate supper around a white-clothed oval table, feet warmed by a charcoal brazier underneath. Over the center of the table hung an imposing brass lamp that only my father lit. I remembered the ritual, seeing him strike a kitchen match and hold it under the gauze mantles, adjusting the flame, concentrating. When it was time for new mantles, he attached twin puckered bags delicately in place, then lit and burned them to a black crisp like moths, dead. A second later they would start to glow to a bright white light—a miracle every time.

A big red-faced man in his sixties appeared in the doorway. He had the look of a farmer, I thought, rather than a shopkeeper. He looked familiar somehow.

I had a clear image of him sitting on a low stool milking one of his two cows and facing me where I'd climbed to watch him from the stone wall between our houses. When I was old enough, he used to hand me the frothing pail over the wall, and I carried it in to our cook. It was Ilyes. His two daughters were near my age and we had played together, though I didn't remember what we had played. I was afraid of those cows.

He identified me—the missionary's daughter—and welcomed me like a true Arab. Then he said, "My first wife was living when I was next door. This one never lived in that house and never knew your family. Also she is young. So you must forgive her for not being more hospitable."

Now she brought in a tray of Arab coffee and sweets, while Ilyes showed us family pictures. One large tinted photograph stood on a starched doily. This was his grandson, George, the only boy in the family. Perhaps we had run into him somehow, since he lived in Detroit, Michigan? A little while later Ilyes asked our daughter's age. He was disappointed that she was eighteen, but she seemed healthy and pretty, he thought. How would we like her to marry their George? We knew it was a compliment.

The old sleeping porch on the second floor held strong memories. We approached the owner of that apartment. To him, as to Ilyes' wife, we were strangers, but he was willing to have us look in.

When I was a child, all four of our white iron beds were rolled out there as soon as we came home from boarding school, and stayed there till we went back to Beirut in the fall. Each bed with its mosquito net and thin white bedspread always stayed in the same location, because the black tar floor softened in the heat and became easily rutted. We wore shoes over to our beds and always shook them out before putting them on again, in case of scorpions. When my friends stayed overnight, we slept on camp cots as close as possible. The rough stucco walls opened to the sky; we looked up at the comforting constellations while someone told "The Pit and the Pendulum" and "The Fall of the House of Usher," with variations.

Most mornings we took sun baths out there, because Mother was a nurse and believed the sun benefited us. I memorized the state capitals on that porch: Bismarck, Pierre, Sacramento, all unreal, all just names learned on the sun porch.

I was telling my husband and children about the state capitals, the stars, the frightening stories, when I heard someone speak to me in Arabic from the doorway, a small dark man with tears in his eyes, "Oh, Munkareet, do you know me?"

It was Aziz, who used to live with his mother next door on

the other side of our house from Ilyes. She was the village dress-maker. She worked on the floor, surrounded by bright snippets of satin and lace from the current trousseau. I had pulled out her basting threads and sewed clothes for my dolls out of her scraps. Aziz, ten years older than I, had worked in the village as a stone mason, so I was barely aware of him as I grew up. He knew who I was, even after thirty-three years, and recognized me from the distance of his mother's old house. I cried with him and we hugged each other. We made a plan to spend a day and have a picnic with our two families at the ruins of Baalbek.

Later that day, as I walked with my husband and children through the village, people came out of their houses and greeted me, begging us to come inside and drink coffee. They told me stories about my father and mother, although more about my father. With his formidable uprightness, it had taken only a little exaggeration to turn him into a myth. My mother they saw as one of them, because she had been born there, a true *bint Arab;* but he was like an Old Testament prophet.

On Sunday we walked to the Protestant church. I remembered how on Easter mornings my father, walking down that street with my mother and us children, would call out in a ringing voice to those we met, "Christ is risen!" The answer would come back, "He is risen indeed." It always embarrassed me.

Inside the church, the whitewashed walls were just as they had been, without ornament except for a tablet on either side of the pulpit, where the Ten Commandments shone in gold. In the back, a small pump organ (perhaps the one my mother had played) stood on a raised platform, and there the choir used to sit. I used to sit there too, to be with her. Once she persuaded me to sing a solo in English, "Voices of Spring," to her accompaniment. I remembered my clammy hands clutching the music as I croaked and whispered it out. We sat there now.

The endless hours on the hard pew every Sunday! It seemed then I could not understand a word of the minister's high Arabic. How was it that now, after all these years, I could understand his words? I heard the minister tell the congregation how greatly the missionary who lived here had loved them and that, in proof of his love, the missionary's daughter was here with them this morning.

Then we sang a hymn, and I remembered the tune was one Mother used to play.

I think of Souk-el-Gharb as I remember it in childhood and as it appeared on my brief return, and I wonder about it now. Recently I asked the owner of a Middle Eastern bakery in Chicago what word he might have of the village.

He said it had long been in the hands of the Shiite militia, and villagers had all been forbidden access.

I turned away; but a second Lebanese, overhearing my question and wanting to comfort me with a softer answer, said, "Oh, don't worry. The villagers are free to come and go as they wish. Besides, you know how the Lebanese are. The day after the bombing, they'd be in there cleaning up the rubble and rebuilding the streets and houses, replanting their vineyards and gardens."

These stories about Lebanon are my way of cleaning up rubble, rebuilding streets and houses, replanting vineyards and gardens.

The Color Red

Most of what I remember happened in Souk-el-Gharb, where we moved when I was five, but I was three and we were still living in my first house, the stone manse in Zahleh.

I had a drinking glass. It was like the glasses on our table but small; it fit my hand. It was new and special to me, too special to let anyone else touch it. I went to the kitchen to wash it.

It must have been mid-afternoon. I pushed through the heavy swinging door to the kitchen, huge, dark and gloomy as a cave and empty. Keffa had put away the food and washed everything, ending with the floor, and now she had climbed the back stairs to embroider and take a nap. As I went in I smelled wet stone floor. I dragged Keffa's chair over to the head-high sink and climbed up, glad she wasn't here to insist on helping. I washed my glass carefully, as I'd watched Keffa do, rinsed it, and jumped down. Then I ran with my wet glass back toward the swinging door and the dining room, where my mother and father were having tea.

Then I was slipping, falling, my glass still in my right hand, holding tight to it, so it would be all right. I heard the crash it made. I clutched what was left, trying to save it. I saw my beautiful glass, smashed. Then I noticed some of the glass pieces were red and some were sitting in puddles of red, and the puddles were growing. The hand that held the glass felt hot and funny. Red stuff was running down to my elbow.

Father gathered me up and Mother ran to get something. Keffa came down from her nap and reached past Father's arms to me. She was making wailing noises. Father told her to be quiet.

There was an enormous white bundle around my hand. My

27

Zahleh, 1927

father carried me and I carried my white bundle, cradling it like a doll. Father pelted, slipped and slid down the dirt steps that led from the manse, down to the center of Zahleh.

And then we were in Dr. Jerisatti's office-dining room. He had me sit on the edge of his dark dining room table. He stood in front of me, in his striped suit and vest with the watch chain that reached across his stomach. He unwrapped my bundle, though I tried to hold on to it. He said in Arabic over my head to my father, who stood at my back, one hand on each of my shoulders, "I will have to sew it. It will just take a minute."

I watched while he opened a glass-fronted dish cabinet to his right and got out a needle and thread. He put the end of the thread in his mouth and threaded the needle just the way our sewing woman did. He was a man. How did he know how to do that? He began to sew my hand. He sewed for a long time, pricking and pulling, and pressing the cut parts together. I began to scream and my father held me against him, trying to keep me from pulling away from Dr. Jerisatti's needle. I felt shaking and I couldn't tell if it was me or Father. I think it was both of us.

The doctor called to Mrs. Jerisatti in the parlor and she came in, in her Sunday dress. It was blue and shiny with beads sewn on like flowers. The look on her face said, *No babies allowed here!* She gripped my legs so I couldn't kick anymore.

I was very tired. I stopped struggling and closed my eyes. But even behind my eyes I saw red, red oriental rugs and dark red wood and the blood. Fear. Fury. I hated them all, but especially Dr. Jerisatti.

Then when it didn't matter anymore, my father carried me home, back up the hill to my mother.

For several days I was told over and over how brave I had been. Dr. Jerisatti remained a villain for me. Later, when my hand swelled up and had to be soaked and lanced, Mother said bitterly that he probably had not disinfected the needle. I was pampered like a princess and praised as a heroine. Father didn't tell about my screaming.

The scar is still here on my right ring finger, trailing down into my palm. The middle joint is a little fatter than normal, and the last joint will not bend by itself. If it is true that our bodies hold the memory of all our past experiences, then that one fattened finger is where all the memory of this is stored.

The Mulberry Juice Dress

It was Sunday again. The stone stairs leading up from church toward the manse seemed steeper and more dizzying in the dry sirocco air. I climbed, dragging on my father's hand.

"Old Lady," he said, "either you're going to have to grow longer legs or these steps are going to have to be lowered."

I cherished "Old Lady," and for that I would gladly grow my legs longer, immediately, if possible. Anything to show him what I could do, anything to make him proud of me. Perhaps today, this afternoon, the chance would come to do my poem. I felt a twinge of excitement, then fright.

When we stopped to rest, Mother and the boys caught up. Mother was wearing her summer Sunday dress that was my favorite, white cambric with blue bands around the neck and wrists and around the hem at her ankles. She'd taken off her straw hat and stuck the hat pin through the crown; now as she rested she fanned herself with it. Her hair stuck and unstuck in little tendrils. Arthur and Philip steamed in their knickers and white Sunday shirts.

My father picked me up and put me on his back, careful to smooth down my starched dress, so it would not crumple or show my legs too much. Trickles of sweat started down from his hair into his Sunday collar. If I hitched up a bit, I could wipe off the sweat, a bit more and I could lick it. I did. Salty, quite good. Father didn't stop me as I'd half expected he would: *Now that you are four, Margaret . . .*

Philip ran on ahead, giving my foot nearest him a sharp yank as he passed. "Little baby!" he muttered.

I pretended not to feel it and looked around from my high place, playing I was on a camel. Across the city, I saw the dome

31

Zahleh, 1926
Anna has been added, and I'm not sure we should keep her.

and *muezzin's* tower of Zahleh's biggest mosque, around it a quilt of flat mud roofs with a few slanted red tile roofs of rich people's houses. I liked the flat roofs, because most of them had lean-tos of leafy boughs where the whole family slept, now that nights were hot. If our family had one on our roof, would I have to go to bed first or would we all go to bed at the same time? If Philip went to bed at the same time I did, he'd probably tease me.

Trays of thyme, sumac, and sesame were drying on the flat roofs. Soon the mothers and grandmothers would stir and pound the herbs together to be sprinkled over bread and goat cheese. Each family thought its *zahtar* was the best, and our friends brought us samples so we could eat some too. Here and there bright orange squares of apricot paste dried on trays among the green browns of the herbs.

On Sundays, after church, that was tiresome, and dinner, that was good, there was company. No telling ahead of time what that would be like. If the visitors didn't bring their children along, I had to stay, wearing my Sunday dress, in the parlor with the grownups. If I didn't listen, I at least had to be quiet.

Lucky Arthur and Philip. They got to put on old clothes after Sunday dinner and go out with their new goats, pushing them around with short sticks and pretending to be goatherds. I was too young to have a goat, my mother said, and anyway the boys needed to be like other boys and become brown and healthy.

On their side of the parlor, the men talked about the government being like a giant who doesn't pay any attention to people in trouble, but who might pounce when you weren't looking. They liked to talk about cars, and always asked after the Ford the church in Illinois had given us. The cluster of women would be quiet, or would make polite compliments. When women visited my mother without the men around, they often cried and whispered behind their handkerchiefs about their children's health or their husbands' ways; with the men here, the women were all smiles and flutters.

Sometimes visitors brought their children and we could play, although some children stuck to their mothers on the parlor couch, so they might just as well not have come. Today it began with no children and with me sitting stiffly on the couch by my mother, like the shy children. I was supposed to help entertain Mr. and Mrs. Hajjar. The Hajjars had children but seldom brought them along, although everyone said they were very good, very intelligent, and very well behaved. The last time Father and Mother came back from calling on the Hajjars, they told me about Selwa's sewing.

"She's only thirteen," my mother told me, "but we saw her trousseau, nearly finished already. You should have seen her embroidered bureau runners."

Ahzeem Hajjar, her eight-year-old brother, sang a love song for the guests. My father said, "The neighbors all whispered he had the voice of a nightingale."

I was disappointed I hadn't been there to hear him. "Was his voice really like a nightingale, Father?"

Father snorted. "Oh, his voice was fine, I suppose, but the song wasn't nice. I said as much to the Hajjars when the song was over. I had thought better of them than that."

When I was partway out the door, I overheard my mother say, "Will, I thought Ahzeem's song was dear. I do wish you didn't always feel you had to speak your mind. Sometimes it's quite embarrassing."

Father used his church voice. "It's a matter of principle for us as American missionaries to act as examples. I wish you'd be more of a helpmeet to me at such times, Elizabeth."

That part I didn't understand, even though I heard the words. I did understand, though, that when the Hajjars visited, Father would want me to do something he could be proud of in front of them. I counted on the new poem I'd learned to be just the right thing. I felt especially pleased with myself because the poem was the hardest I'd ever learned. The Arabic was full of rolled *r*'s and *gh*'s in the back of my throat, and it was fun once I'd learned it. I'd been practicing with Keffa, sitting on her lap in the kitchen, every day for the past week. Every time I got a new line right, Keffa would squeeze me to her feather-comforter breast, and there'd be a whiff of attar of roses.

Once, when Keffa was telling me about her family back in the village, she ended up laughing that her father named her Keffa ("that's enough"). "There were six sisters before me," she said. "How was he to find husbands for so many girls? So after I was born he named me Keffa, and then there were no more children."

I was impressed at how Keffa's father let God know his opinion. He sounded a lot like my father.

I had a startling thought. "Keffa, what if your father had named one of the others Keffa? Then she'd have been the last and you'd never have been born or come to live with us." Which led me to another unthinkable thought: "I hope he never finds you a husband."

Keffa laughed and squeezed me, and said that was in God's hands. Then she taught me the poem that she learned when she was my age. It said:

I'm a little girl, don't think I'm a big girl.
I went up on the roof and the wind blew me.
I went to the doctor and he gave me medicine.
I said to him, "What is this medicine?"
He said, "Almonds and filberts and cake-of-the-wind."

Now my father was asking me if there were something I could recite for Mr. and Mrs. Hajjar. So I stood up and began:

Anna bint zaghaira, lat khumnoony kabaira.
Ruht ahl satah, le deffni il howah.
Ruht ahl doctor, wa suffni dowah.
Iltillu, "Shu hal dowah?"
Al'lee, "Fistuh' wa binduh' wa kahk-el-howah."

I floundered between the *fistuh'* and the *binduh'* on the last line and struggled to get it back, but my mind was a blank. I dared a look at my father, who simply looked back at me with no words but a tight mouth. My mother smiled, though, and the Hajjars clapped delicately and said I could be taken for an Arab.

Keffa came in with a tray of Arab coffee for the company, and I passed ginger snaps. Keffa mouthed to me, "How did the poem go?" I made a face. I knew there was something I'd done wrong, besides muddling the end of the poem.

The next callers were Dr. and Mrs. Jerisatti and their daughters, Uhmar, five, and Shemsi, three. I fit between them in age. I could hardly wait to get out and play in the yard, away from the grown-ups and the reciting of poems. Most especially, I didn't want to look at Dr. Jerisatti. He was the one who had sewn up my hand. He'd hurt me a lot. Mrs. Jerisatti had held me hard by the legs so I couldn't kick. She was just as bad. I kept my eyes down and edged toward the door, waiting for Shemsi and Uhmar. But there they stood in their matching sailor dresses, white ribbed stockings, and patent leather shoes, between their not-to-be-looked-at parents in the parlor, as rooted and silent as four trees.

When I got to the door I looked back and saw that, quietly and sedately, the two girls were coming. Slowly, through the door and out into the still, hot air they came. And then we were racing to the far end of the garden, where the mulberry trees made a dark jungle.

Uhmar climbed a mulberry first, with me and Shemsi right behind her. There was a larger mulberry tree we moved to, a tree that made itself easily into an apartment house with living space for each of us, with leaves for dishes and mulberries for food. The mulberries were very ripe and ready to fall at a touch; the ground was purple with them.

We didn't need to talk. We looked at each other and began pulling off our irritating Sunday dresses, frilled slips and underpants, shoes, and finally white ribbed stockings. My only qualm was about the underpants. When Arthur and Philip and I had our sun baths every morning, we kept ours on. But underwear would spoil it all.

Free, we began to paint ourselves and each other with mulberry juice. I began at my neck, covering my arms to the wrists and my legs to my ankles. It was a beautiful dark red-purple dress.

Shemsi made a dotted dress for herself, some of the dots like suns with rays coming out all around, because her name meant sun. She painted short scalloped sleeves on herself, needing a little help to do the backs of her arms. Uhmar decided on a pattern of crescent moons, because her name meant moon. Shemsi and I did the crescents on the backs of her legs and on her back, except where she wanted the neck scooped in a daring low cut. When we were done, we admired ourselves and each other and went back to our tree apartment.

Keffa found us there. She slapped her hand over her mouth, turned around and hurried back into the house, clutching her white apron. A few moments later she was back, drying her eyes with one corner of her apron. My mother was there with her, laughing. Then I saw Mother turn to Keffa, saw them put their arms around each other with their foreheads touching, holding each other up while they laughed. My father was nowhere to be seen, but the Jerisattis came out and stood stiff and speechless, looking at the transformed Shemsi and Uhmar.

Keffa straightened up and smoothed her apron. "Excuse me, and excuse the children," she said to Mrs. Jerisatti. "Let me bathe Shemsi and Uhmar along with Margaret. See, it will not take a minute. I'm going to get the basin now." She brought out one of the zinc tubs from the wash house, filling it from the cistern. "I can do three as easily as one," she said.

My mother said, "Please let the children enjoy a bath together. It's nothing really. They have done nothing wrong."

The Jerisattis had a whispered conference and then talked to Mother, shaking their heads. She went into the house and came back with a sheet for each of the girls. Uhmar pulled hers up over her head and drew a fold across her face to her eyes, like a Bedouin woman. Shemsi watched and did the same, and they giggled to each other. Their mother hustled them out the gate without looking back. Dr. Jerisatti walked a few paces behind in a dignified way.

Good-bye, Shemsi and Uhmar, I said with my eyes, while Keffa soaped and scrubbed me. First I sat in the tub, then I stood outside the tub, while Keffa poured pails of water over me. I watched the purple red froth diminish to pink froth, then pale pink, then clear water, soaking into the hard dry ground.

My mother went to the gate to see the Jerisattis off, then came back into the yard and dried me with an old towel. It seemed to me she did it particularly gently. I looked at her face and saw that she looked sad, now that she'd stopped laughing. She said, "Your father wants to talk to you in his study, Margaret. I'm afraid he's very disappointed with you."

"Come in," said my father when I knocked.

I had hoped he wouldn't hear and that somehow I would be reprieved. But I didn't know yet from what. He sat at his desk, his chair swivelled around to face the chair I was in.

"Margaret," he said after the long silence that always came first. "Let's start with your little poem. Did you know what it said, the one you recited this afternoon?"

I did know what the poem said, I thought. I went through the lines saying the words over.

"Was there some other meaning, something I didn't know, like Ahzeem's love song that wasn't nice?" I asked my father.

"No, no, it wasn't that," he said. "The poem was just an Arabic tongue-twister, like Peter Piper. Mother tells me you've been learning it from Keffa all week, so that means you spent a lot of time and effort on it."

I thought: *He's saying I spent all that time on a silly poem, and then I didn't even get it all right. I must be stupid. He's being patient with me.*

My father went on, and I heard his voice get louder and tighter. A vein in his forehead and another in the side of his neck puffed out. I heard him, but in fragments: "time . . . limited time . . . time on earth . . . wasted time . . ." My father's words were as hard to comprehend as this morning's sermon in high Arabic. I sat up straighter in my chair and fixed my eyes on him to show I was paying attention.

"Right now I'm very disappointed in you, Margaret. I want you to be a credit to me."

That I understood very well.

"Next time, Margaret, why don't you try learning something from the Bible, or even from the Koran, instead of spending time on nonsense verse."

He paused and I thought maybe it was over. I started to slide off my chair.

Then he said, "As for that performance with the mulberry juice, I can't think what got into you." He stared at me angrily, started to say something, but stopped himself. "I can't really talk to you about that part, Margaret; it upsets me too much. I'll have to ask your mother to deal with it."

He waited for me to explain in some way so that he could forgive me. And I did want him to forgive me, to call me Old Lady again. But how could I explain? How could I tell him so he would understand about the mulberry juice dress?

Bath Night

On Saturday nights Father came to the supper table in creamy rayon pajamas that stuck damply to his chest and arms. His face glowed pink, beaded with sweat, his eyes bloodshot. Now that he had come, Keffa hurried in from the kitchen with the soup tureen and set it on an Arab straw trivet, waiting in place before him. *"Nahamen!"* she murmured, to bless and congratulate him on his bathed state.

"Allah yinham halakey," he answered, always correct and formal with the response. She looked down at her forearms, wound up tight in her apron.

Father beamed his benevolence out at the rest of us. My heart responded as though to the sun on the first beach day. He'd cut and cleaned his nails. The skin of his fingers was wrinkled and the hairs on the backs of his hands stood up crisply.

Looking toward bath night, he had spent this afternoon sweeping out the hen house, sending up dusty clouds of straw and putting down fresh straw. He'd dressed for the job in a collarless shirt, buttoned up to the neck and to the wrists, tucked into droopy pants, and on his head a handkerchief knotted at each corner. Just before he went into the chicken house he'd put a clothes pin on his nose. Like all his chores, this one had been done in a frenzy of thoroughness, scraping stubborn lumps off the floor, cleaning off the perches and washing the windows, though the chickens hardly seemed to notice. They were, after all, no ordinary chickens but Plymouth Rocks, descendants of the original three hens and a rooster who came out to Lebanon with us on the freighter our last furlough.

To hatch their eggs, my father ordered an incubator and set

41

it up in the pantry between the dining room and kitchen, where it had the presence of a grand piano. It was as exciting as getting a Montgomery Ward package to watch through the glass panel for the eggs to begin rocking, and then to listen for the first peep. I would be glued there, seeing the deformed chicks, the late ones that stayed in their broken eggs or tottered out with shell clinging to them, fall down on their useless twigs.

As for my mother, chickens did not belong in the house, except roasted, on a platter. The incubator, with its pervasive acrid smell so near the dining room, offended her beyond words, but Father was undeterred.

"I plan to change the chicken population of Lebanon," he said to my mother as he gave away chicks. She didn't question what he was doing, but she didn't join in either the work involved or the excitement. When we made trips around the countryside and saw Plymouth Rocks, stolid and sensible as shopkeepers, standing by the roadside, not hysterically crossing in front of us as their scrawny white sisters did, my father nodded to the owners or honked his horn, pleased, as we drove on. No comment from Mother.

There was always work to do before the bath. There was the garden to weed, to hoe, and to water carefully by the pailful since there was never water to waste. There was goat manure, bought dry and stored in kerosene cans, to which water had to be added, so it could be poured safely on his beloved tuberoses. Thus dissolved, the goat manure looked like lumpy Arab coffee.

Once I overheard my brother Philip say to Arthur, "I'll drink a demitasse of that stuff if you'll pay me a Syrian pound."

Arthur got the most allowance and saved it; Philip was always looking for get-rich-quick plans. If my father overheard this kind of haggling, he would deliver a sermon on the importance of honest work for honest pay, or honest work which was its own reward and needed no pay. Father, all this time, would have worked up a good sweat carrying pails of water to his dahlias and geraniums.

I did not like the dahlias and geraniums. I considered the

dahlias coarse and the geraniums sappy, but the two old rose bushes, my favorites, got no attention from him at all. The roses were small and fragrant, often wormy. They offered themselves to me to be pulled apart, their petals stuck to my mouth to make Clara Bow lips. They survived and had a special place in my heart because Father considered them not "worthwhile."

One spring morning my father turned over most of the garden, digging and hoeing all day till bath time.

My mother tried to talk to him from the edge of the ruined garden. "What are you *doing*, Will?"

He barely looked at her. He proceeded to plant alfalfa, explaining to me as he did that alfalfa was known to be good for chickens. I was flattered that he was talking to me, but torn at the same time out of loyalty to Mother. I knew she cherished the garden and her view down to Beirut and the sea from the summer house. There the village women would come by with their offerings of needlework, straw mats and baskets, or family troubles—a husband who drank or a child with boils. Eventually, of course, she ignored the alfalfa as she had the chickens and incubator, and talked to the women in the summer house as before, only now she would turn her chair the other way.

Father's happiest moments came when he was working at something worthwhile. He spent hours making checker boards, though he called them lap boards and said they were to write on. Secretly, though it was no secret to us, he loved games and had had very little chance to play as a child. Once he made us a wooden crokinole board with hand-turned counters, a game without educational uses. We loved it for that very reason. When he produced a wooden egg, without a lathe and only hand tools, he needed to have Mother use it as a darning egg to give it dignity. That he had produced a beautiful, deceptively simple, polished egg for the challenge and enjoyment alone was not something to be admitted. Mother continued to use the old wooden darner with a handle she had always used. My father took his egg away and I never saw it again.

I felt sad for Father and critical of Mother, both feelings unusual. Now as I see them in my mind's eye and hear their voices with my adult ears, I wonder if they were in fact having a coded dialogue. I play with the idea:

His message: *See, I have spent months making you this egg. Will you forgive me for the chickens and for making you live with chicken smell and mess?*

And her message back: *You don't fool me. You made that wooden egg for your own enjoyment, not for mine. The egg is not enough. No.*

With all this thinking about my father's nature and what was admissible pleasure for him, I ask myself: *Did he enjoy his Saturday night bath?*

Well, of course. He had worked hard so he deserved it. And besides, he washed away a lot of old sin along with his sweat and dirt. Yes, he enjoyed it.

Picnic

My deviled eggs fit neatly in the English biscuit box Mother found in the pantry. Some of the whites were frayed and the insides had some lumps—the mustard probably—but they looked quite nice all lined up. Sixteen of them. No, I dropped one. Fifteen. I closed the lid and set the box flat in the bottom of the picnic hamper. On top of the biscuit box Mother put a linen dishtowel, its opposite corners tied to make a bag for the figs and grapes. All around she tucked Arab bread, still warm, filled with black olives and goat's cheese sprinkled with *zahtar*. This year's supply of *zahtar* hadn't been made yet, because the thyme was still drying and hadn't been mixed with sesame and sumac. That would smell even better. On top Mother laid another dishtowel.

Our big old green thermos of lemonade stood by the front door, where Father would see it and remember to prop it between two of our feet after Arthur and Philip and I settled in the back seat. Father stowed his rifle in by the picnic basket and blanket, and walked whistling to the front of the car. He poured a little more gasoline into the tank from a five-gallon can. He opened the radiator cap and looked in. Just to be safe, he took a look into the wooden box he'd made for the running board, to be sure all his tire-mending gear was there. I tried to get a window seat but Arthur and Philip had them first.

"All aboard?" Father checked with Mother, sitting in the front passenger seat with Anna on her lap. She nodded. "Everyone been to the bathroom?" He looked piercingly in the car window at me. If I hadn't, he would know it just the way he knew everything about me. I nodded, glad I'd remembered. He climbed into the driver's seat, looked over the cluster of village boys, and picked out Haleem to turn the crank. A cough or two and the motor caught. Haleem straightened, red-faced and proud to have been successful so quickly. He stepped back and herded the others out of the way. Father drove out the iron gate, waving back over his head to the boys. Haleem probably thought he'd have a driving lesson soon, or at least a ride.

Through Souk-el-Gharb and on to the Abeye road we met no other cars. Then a taxi came toward us, full of sightseers, singing and waving, their driver beaming a mouthful of gold as he grazed us and passed.

Father gritted his teeth. "I could smell the *arak* on his breath. I'd like to report him and have his license taken away."

Arak smelled like licorice. I was sorry to have missed it, but I would never say that out loud. Everyone kept quiet as the road dust settled. Father calmed down. After the terraces of grapes and figs came dry rocky land where broom took over. A flock of sheep moved slowly across the road, the shepherd walking dreamily along in their midst like one of them. Father honked and drove as close as he dared, revving his motor and looking fiercely out the side. The herder poked some of the broad wooly backs with a short stick.

"We are all sheep in the sight of Allah," he said smoothly.

Father gripped the wheel.

"We'll get there, Will," Mother said putting a hand on his sleeve.

To fill time Arthur and Philip pulled their slingshots from their knickers' back pockets and checked their condition. I looked on and thought about when to bring up the matter of a slingshot to Father. I had asked him a while ago, but he had just mumbled. Today would have been a good time, the way it started out, but what with the drunk driver and now the wait for the sheep, he might just huff at me. Better to wait a little.

My brothers opened and inspected the ammunition in each of their Quaker Oats boxes.

"We could count them and see," Philip said.

"Well, I'm sure I have more," Arthur said. "Anyway, there

isn't any room to count them in here."

Then he noticed me watching and handed his box to me. "Here. Which one is heavier, mine or Philip's?"

I took my time, lifting first his, then Philip's, giving myself time to register each on my invisible scale. I could feel the greater weight of Philip's mud balls. I'd thought I would. I stalled. I rolled my lips out the way Mother had when she'd tasted the lemonade this morning. Then I put both boxes down on the car floor in front of me and lifted their tops.

The flock of sheep was finally across and Father gunned his motor, dirt shooting out behind.

"Come on, Margaret, which one's heavier?" Philip said. "We aren't going to wait all day."

I wasn't going to be hurried. "You've got more marbles in here and they're bigger, so of course your box weighs more. But . . ." I slowed to be sure they took this in, "but Arthur made his rounder and solider, so they'll probably hit the mark better." Well, now they were both mad at me, but I'd had my moment.

We rounded a curve and caught the first look at the Sleeping Giant, the long descending hills that made a head, chest and bulging stomach, with knees and feet pointing toward Beirut. In winter the figure was blanketed with snow; now it was brown with scrubby trees like rags of clothes. Anna, too young to remember, found and pointed at each part as she discovered it. I was too grown up for that, but no picnic trip to the pines was complete without finding the Giant. I craned my neck to look back at him for as long as possible. To think that an upheaval in the molten core was what formed mountains. Father had told me about that and I mused over molten core, loving the words but unsure of the meaning. Like a hot boiled egg with the white cooling and the yellow still steamy and runny in the middle? I unfocused my eyes so the outlines of the Giant blurred. I imagined an outline that moved, reversing its ups and downs, the whole thing smoking, its shape altered completely. I could only hold it a second, then it went back to the shape I knew—peaceful, unchanging.

We got to Abeye and drove slowly down its main street, empty except for dogs and a few toddlers playing in the ditch, watched over by old women. On the other side of the village, the pine woods waited and I caught my first wave of lovely smell. Father drove us bumpily off the road and into the shade.

Out of the car, I kicked off my shoes to feel the pine needles slide and prick. Arthur and Philip started chasing each other on an obstacle course between the boulders, while Father and Mother debated the right spot to put down the blanket. Anna had dropped off to sleep right after she saw the Sleeping Giant, so Father laid her in the shade to one side.

My mother opened the basket. "Margaret, we forgot the tablecloth! Now the picnic won't be perfect."

I knew how she felt. At the same time, her saying that to me made me feel we were two women having to deal with this problem. I stretched the top dishtowel out as smooth as I could in the middle of the blanket to act as a tablecloth and began arranging food. Last of all came the biscuit box with my deviled eggs. I opened it carefully.

"Oh, they look perfect," Mother said, taking one and passing the box on to Philip. She handed around bread and olives. I saw Philip look over his deviled egg.

"Yup, perfect all right. Gray deviled eggs." I stuck my tongue out at him behind my napkin. He probably wanted to throw his egg away, but he'd be wasting food. When he gagged over a piece of eggshell, he threw the rest away and gave me a look of triumph.

I saw my mother reach for another egg. "Delicious," she said.

When everyone was through eating, Father wiped the ends of his moustache and walked over to the car. He came back with his rifle and cartridges.

Mother looked up. "Oh, Will, must you?" She sounded as if once more everything was not going to be perfect. "I thought we would have a lovely quiet family time together. Besides, Anna's still sleeping."

"Just a little target practice, Elizabeth. I'll take the boys on out to the clearing over there and you'll hardly hear us."

Anna stirred hearing her name. She opened her eyes and saw the rifle.

"Can I shoot too? I want a turn." She got to her feet to get ready.

Father laughed the way he often did at what Anna said, calling her Husti ("my share"). "Wait a bit and grow a bit. You're not even big enough to carry this gun, let alone aim it."

I walked up to where he held it lightly balanced across his arm and took hold of it. It was heavy, but I managed to heave it up to my shoulder as I'd seen him do. "See? It's not too heavy for me. I'm big enough now."

I marched a few steps as the guards did around the government house in Beirut, knees high, the gun straight up against my shoulder.

Philip grasped the gun by the barrel and pulled it sharply away. "Guns aren't for girls, silly. Don't you know anything?"

I reached for the gun, but Philip stretched it high out of my reach. I pulled hard on his shirt, then clawed his neck. He laughed at me and kept his hold on the gun. Usually, by now Father or Mother would interrupt and tell whoever was squabbling to stop it. I was in the right. It was just a matter of time.

I looked to my mother. She said, "I brought your needles and yarn to do a little knitting, if you like. Why don't we go over there and sit in the shade."

In the same moment I saw my father turn away with the boys, Philip still carrying the rifle, heading for the clearing where they could put up their target.

"Wait for me. I want to come too," I called. Then louder, "Wait for me!" Couldn't they hear?

No answer.

"Father!"

He kept walking.

I stood still looking after them, while behind me my mother settled herself on the blanket. From a corner of my eye I saw knitting needles and a ball of bright pink yarn laid out for me.

In the clearing Arthur was holding a paper target up to a tree and looking over his shoulder as Father sighted.

"Up a little higher," he shouted and Arthur moved it up and held it, while Philip hammered in nails, top and bottom. Then the three of them stood in a row behind a line drawn in the sand, and I saw Arthur take the rifle and aim. His shot went wide. He scuffed at the dirt with his toe and Father said something like, "That was all right for a first go." Philip took the rifle for his turn.

No use watching. I began to walk away, not back to my mother and Anna but away—out of sight and sound of everyone. No one must see me if I was going to cry. I just wouldn't cry.

The gunshots went off at regular intervals. Between shots I felt my heart drumming, my skull expanding as though I were in a great dust storm, everything around me a blur, in the middle my hot self—molten.

I whispered to myself, *I'm eight years old. I can't be doing this.* I could hear Mother saying, "Margaret, you're all through having those terrible tantrums you used to have. Don't start again. You're too old for that."

I sucked in some long breaths and wiped my eyes. I looked around, then down, hoping to find something to hang on to.

At my feet the pine needles moved. I crouched to get a closer look. A black ant was making its way through the pine needles, nudging under, climbing over, falling, starting off again. Another followed, then another. A file of them was coming out of the small neat hole at the top of their hill. Sand sifted down the slope from the traffic of ants.

I heard another gunshot. I attended the ants. Doing that seemed to calm me down. I cleared a path in the pine needles to make their move easier, carried a few at a time to wherever they were going. I found a stick and collected a few ants on it, but they kept dropping off.

Another shot, followed by the clicking of cartridges being

emptied onto the ground. I took my stick in my fist and began jabbing, slowly at first, then faster and deep into the sand. The stick broke. I used the sharp broken end, then flung it away. No good. I found a thicker one and got back to work. There were a lot of ants. They'd given up all order and scurried erratically in different directions. Methodically, I stopped one after the other with a single hard twist.

A green-black scarab beetle came into the execution place. I hesitated for just a moment, seeing his beauty and remembering him from what Grandpa had told me. Then I skewered him through his shell, satisfied with the sound it made.

My mother was calling to me—something about a daisy chain—did I want to show Anna how to make one? I didn't answer, kept on jabbing, collecting the small curled bodies and fragments into a pile, along with the beetle carcass.

It had been a while since I'd heard the rifle. At the clearing my brothers had their slingshots out and were toeing up to a line, facing the torn gun target. Each one's Quaker Oats box stood open at his feet. My father stood behind another line to one side and farther away from the target with his own slingshot.

I heard my mother's footsteps come toward me and stop.

"Margaret, dear," my mother said, "You really must try not to sulk. It's so ugly. Didn't you enjoy helping me with the picnic, and making the deviled eggs all by yourself? I was so proud of you. It's so wonderful to have a little girl for company."

Confession

My sin sat heavily on me. Ever since I'd come home from school in Beirut, I had been going over my sin, trying to belittle it. But sitting in the circle for morning prayers, I knew it hadn't worked. The lumpy brown couch, the Morris chair, and the rocker with Mother's knitting in it should have made me feel safe. Now that the iron stove was out of the parlor for the summer, there was more space opening out to the sun at the windows, but I could barely feel it. My sin invaded everything. My eye fell on the picture of Hope over the couch. There she was, poor blind thing with one string left.

My father read aloud the mission prayer request for this day in the month of June 1932: "Pray for the British island of Socotra, once Christian, now Moslem."

In my state of mind that translated to "Pray for the ten-year-old Margaret, once good, now bad." Yesterday's request, "Pray for the Ahmedi in his darkness and need," had changed to "Pray for Margaret in her darkness and need."

After the prayer for Socotra, there was Bible reading, but we were still in the begats, so nothing connected with me. Then we all knelt in front of our chairs to say personal prayers. If Father were to hear my thoughts this morning, he would get red in the face and that vein in his neck would throb. Arthur would sneer, Philip tease. Anna would keep bringing up the subject—not to tease, but to know more.

What I need, I thought suddenly, *is to confess what I did to Mother. Alone.* She would be the one who could listen to the whole thing and say, "Oh, I see how it was," punish me a little bit and keep me from doing wrong again. My breath came easier.

Father began by clearing his throat and looking up to the wall near the ceiling. "Heavenly Father," he said in his church voice that made me squirm and get goose bumps at the same time. "Heavenly Father, guide me..." but I did not hear the words.

Anna, kneeling next to Father in the circle, clutched her cat, Beesi, under one arm. "Please bless Beesi," she said, "and make her cough go away. I won't give her any more baths."

Arthur snickered. Everyone waited while he sobered. Finally, he asked God in a rush to bless the family. That was always what you said when you couldn't think of anything.

Philip's turn. He sighed. "Please help me with the algebra I have to make up this summer." God must know all about that, but it was safest to specify.

Mother said, "Dear Jesus, please help Latifi. She's so young and her baby is late." Mother knew about anyone who was sick in the village. Sometimes I felt proud about that; sometimes I felt angry, as though Mother had a hundred children instead of four.

I was last in the circle. I thanked God for his help in time of need and I meant it. Mother gave me a startled look and moved over as though to speak to me when we got to our feet, but I hurried away to wait for the right time to be with her, privately and uninterrupted.

My chance came unexpectedly that Sunday. The walk along the Kayfoon road, the one we always took on Sunday afternoons, turned out to be a walk with just Mother. My father had driven off on mission business; with him away, my brothers were safe to visit a friend, and Anna asked to stay home and look after Beesi.

I had my mother alone, but now I didn't know how to start. I looked over at her for some reassurance as we left our gate—at her soft flowered dress, her lisle stockings, her black tie-shoes with Cuban heels. Her face was already brown. She wore her soft, thin hair coiled in a figure eight, filled out by a switch from Montgomery Ward. This was a secret she had told me, a secret never to tell outside the family. She said I could have the old switch when the new one came. That occupied my thoughts for a while. I pictured myself and my two best friends taking turns with it, pushing big tortoise shell hairpins into it as my mother did, and putting a hat on top. I thought of how she trusted me with her secret, just as I would trust her with mine in a minute.

With that thought, I took a deep breath, ready to start. Just then my mother said, "How I love this time of day when the light changes and the air cools."

It would be rude of me to interrupt her. I waited for my moment to come.

We walked beyond the last house in our village and now on either side were terraced vineyards and fig trees, the terraces on the right sloping toward the coast. Wild broom and clumps of daisies pushed out between the terraces and along the road.

"Let's take some home, shall we? At least the daisies," Mother said. "The stems are probably too tough on the broom. If only Father were here, he'd have his knife."

But if Father were here I couldn't talk to Mother. I thought, *When we get to the edge of Kayfoon, I'll tell her.* We picked all the daisies we could hold.

At the outskirts of the village we began to hear frenzied barking. Someone must have thrown out a few scraps so the mongrels that patrolled the streets were fighting. We stopped and turned around, walking quickly, not looking back.

The barking died away. Mother said, slowing to catch her breath, "Father always carries a stick when we come this way. I was frightened."

I was afraid of the dogs too, but even more I was afraid of my sin and of putting off the telling any longer.

"Mother, I want to tell you something," I said. No stopping now. "Do you remember how I told you Danny Stewart and I played the story of *The Mill on the Floss* in English class? He was Tom and I was Maggie Tulliver."

"Yes?" said my mother, looking at her daisies and pulling

out dead stems as she walked.

"Well, he had to say he loved me in the scene we acted, and all the other fourth-graders yelled and stamped. Remember?"

My mother nodded. I knew I was taking too long.

"When we went out to recess, he told me it was true. Not just in the play, I mean." (Easy so far. Now comes the hard part.) "After that, he asked me if I wanted to show him my thing and he'd show me his. And we did." There—I'd told it all.

I waited for Mother to answer.

"Where?" my mother asked.

"Oh, in the fourth-grade room. Everyone had left and it was dark."

I remembered chalk dust and the smell of wet blackboards, the dim shapes of chairs upended on the desks, the sound along the hall of the janitor's mop swish and pail rattle.

As though my mother had been there too, listening for sounds, she said now, "Did anyone see you? The janitor? Any one of the teachers?"

"No, no one."

"You took an awful chance."

"I know. I was so nervous I didn't really look. I was too afraid somebody would catch us, but no one did."

I waited. Mother smiled, then laughed.

"How did you manage with those bloomers?"

The last thing I had expected from my mother was laughter. What did my bloomers have to do with it? Mother had the dressmaker sew them, a pair to match each school dress. "What is it? What are you laughing about?"

My mother stopped laughing and stood still. "I'm sorry, dear. I wasn't laughing about the bloomers."

We walked in silence for a while. I couldn't seem to breathe right. What about what I had done, my sin?

My mother said, "You've been worried about this, haven't you?"

I waited for whatever she would say, probably that what I'd

done was disgusting and shameful. If she did say that, there would be an inner *Yes*, my mother confirming what I believed. It would be like feeling funny and hot, and my mother saying, "Yes, you do have a fever." My mother continued silent, but I felt sure of what her next words would be, that I needed an enema. I would hate that, but at least then it would all be over.

I looked at my mother and saw that she was laughing again.

"I got to thinking about Danny's father," she said. She might not have been talking to me at all, but to one of her grown-up friends. "Professor Stewart's always so self-righteous about university children, compared to mission children, when it comes to problems."

We were almost at our gate.

She said, "Wait till he hears about his own Danny at the next Community School board meeting. I can't wait to see his face."

No dogs had followed us. Mother turned at our gate and stood to watch the last of the sun. I looked at her. Her face was gleeful and she'd clearly forgotten all about me. At that moment my mother might as well have been alone.

I longed to break in and shake her and say, "Listen, Mother, I told you about Danny and me so you'd know how bad I was. That was the main thing, but you haven't said anything about that. And how dare you talk about my secret to Danny's father, anyway?" I didn't say it.

I felt my mother reach over to give me a squeeze and I backed off, pretending to hurry to get the daisies in water. Mother followed me into the house.

I headed down the dark hall to the kitchen toward the dim light of the kerosene lamps. I smelled them along with *kousa* soup (Arab squash) bubbling on the puffer.

I put the daisies in a pail of water and chose vases from the pantry, setting them in a row beside me. I arranged and rearranged the daisies.

Then, on impulse, I went over to the stove and ladled a

scalding spoonful into my mouth.

The pain was so intense, I dropped the spoon and screamed. But at that moment, I had the punishment I was looking for and I forgot my disappointed heart.

Arabic Lessons

"Illiteracy is a scourge like cholera or typhus," my father used to say. Once he called it "a spreading tide that must be stemmed," and for a while I pictured it red like blood, or yellow like pus. My heart responded to the passion and intensity he usually saved for the pulpit. Father began to stem the tide of illiteracy, crisscrossing Syria in our Model T and then the Model A, examining schools. But that didn't feel like enough.

Then he and Mother adopted Serghaya, a primitive village in the interior, as their special project. They went from our comfortable familiar house in Souk and lived for weeks at a time in a small mud hut in the village. Mother focused on the matter of the water used for drinking, cooking, and washing—the stream running through Serghaya, shared by the villagers with their cows, donkeys and dogs. She got the women to boil water for drinking, as a start, and later had a fountain put in at the spring so the water could be collected clean.

Father began reading and writing classes for the men, at least those willing to come after their long days in the fields. Classes had to be interesting or entertaining, so the men wouldn't drop off to sleep. How to find the right learning material? School primers were available, but the men seemed to feel sheepish reading from them, and would laugh and poke fun at each other when they read the simple words and sentences aloud. Father brought old newspapers from home, there being no newspaper in their village, and that worked better. Sometimes, as a treat for them and for himself, Father wrote out a story of Jehah, the wise fool who always won in the end.

I began asking Father about his classes whenever he and Mother got back from Serghaya. Mother would have loved to

59

tell about teaching nutrition, infant care, and knitting, but it was about his work I wanted to hear. That was novel for me, to really want to know what he had to tell me. It was probably novel for him to have me be receptive, instead of restless, around him. As we talked I began to recognize some of his star pupils by name. There was the man who supplied Father with new Jehah stories and so had a special place and liked to be called Jehah himself. The new Jehah became inspired to write out stories and then read them to the class. Another man learned to write the names of his large extended family and wrote down fragments of their history.

The summer I was twelve, I decided I wanted Arabic lessons; that is, I wanted to learn to read and write Arabic. Our American school in Beirut didn't require Arabic, or even offer it, though we had French as a matter of course. True, the law probably required it; but, looking back, I think English and French must have been viewed as culturally superior. The question of Arabic as a school subject never came up. But now, after those conversations with my father about the men learning Arabic, I wanted it for myself. And secretly I hoped it would please my father, though I did not voice the thought.

My parents agreed to engage Sitt Miriam Mishahleni to be my teacher. She lived in Shemlan about a mile and a half from our village. I remember walking there, taking the wide curve of dirt road to the near edge of Shemlan. It was a half-hour walk, an hour on hot days, and tedious, except that there were vineyards along the road, and custom said that whatever hung over the road belonged to the traveler. A scramble across the ditch and low stone wall got me a good handful. So on my first trips to class I nibbled green grapes, dipped in salt from a shaker in my pocket.

At the outskirts of Shemlan, I turned off to the lower village, down street-stairs that narrowed at Sitt Miriam's gate into her private cement steps. They were lined with large kerosene cans and smaller round ones, uniformly rusted and planted with marigolds and pansies, with parsley, mint, and oregano. At the bottom of the steps, her house was small and neat, but I was allowed only into the lesson room.

Sitt Miriam was also small, to match her house, I thought. She was solidly plump like a bolster, and I remember her always dressed in dark cotton dresses, in some barely noticeable print, long-sleeved and high-necked. She smelled faintly of sweat and of what she cooked and ate: lamb, onions, oil and thyme, Arab coffee, and gummy sweet Turkish delight. She pulled her dark, tightly curling hair into a bun, but tendrils sprang out without permission. She was in her fifties, I suppose. She taught in the village school during the winters, and tutored in summer to eke out a living. She had heavy eyebrows and ardent deep-set eyes. I do not recall any smiles.

I remember my first class. Sitt Miriam gave me a thick paper-bound primer and a book of lined pages for writing. She sat down next to me in a child's straight chair like mine, and read me the Arabic alphabet slowly, pointing at each letter and making me repeat it after her. When she was satisfied, she would grunt and move her finger to the next letter. I liked the rhyming pairs of letters, soft and hard, or soft and guttural: "Calf-Koff, Tuh-Thuh, Sod-Dod." When Sitt Miriam got to the last four letters, I repeated them, shouted them, with staccato flourish, a new school cheer, *"Hey, Wow, Lam-aleph, Yeh."* Sitt Miriam's mouth tightened, but she let it pass.

Sitt Miriam showed me the vowels, small marks I'd never noticed before, written above or below the consonants. She had me say aloud the sound each consonant took on as a vowel sign was added, and I heard myself making sounds like those that came through the open doors of the village schoolhouse. Now they made sense. I was very excited.

The best part of the lesson came when I could read the first sentence in the primer: *"Deekoo Nurin ma saha heena tarr."* Which is to say, "Nur's rooster didn't crow when he flew." Then I wrote it in my copybook from right to left on the last page, which was the first page for an Arab pupil.

I was to go home and practice the alphabet, read and reread that sentence, write and rewrite it. In those first days, I read the sentence proudly to anyone who came near, and I brought up the subject of literacy, feeling myself adult and serious.

The roadside grapes ripened and I ate them on the way, as I'd eaten the sour ones in the first weeks. After a while, I took longer to walk the Shemlan road. I stopped practicing at home some time after the second lesson. Instead, I counted on my quick ear and fast talk to carry me through.

It didn't, not with Sitt Miriam. She knew a flash in the pan when she saw one, and my guesswork must have been laughable. Not that she laughed. After two classes like that, Sitt Miriam said flat out, "Sitt Margaret, I think you want me to make a hole in the side of your head and spoon the Arabic in. If I could, I would."

I still remember her dark look as she said the words, and I believed she would have very much liked to make a hole in my head, but not to spoon in Arabic. I remember, too, a whiff of Turkish delight, and I thought how sweet that smelled and how mean she was.

Now, I think how she must have struggled to recapture the promise of my first lessons. Then, seeing me slack off, how honorable she was to confront me, even when doing so meant cutting off a small but significant source of income.

I expected and dreaded my parents' response when I told them my Arabic lessons were over. At least, I thought, they'd remind me that I'd wanted the lessons, that I should have known ahead of time that learning to read and write Arabic would be hard, but that it was so worthwhile. I imagined Father saying, "Don't you know I need you to fight illiteracy here at home, Margaret, while I fight it in the field?" Instead, he said, "Then I guess we shouldn't waste the money."

My mother stopped counting stitches on the neck of the newest sweater and said from her rocker: "I think trying to study Arabic when it's so hot is just too much. It really is just as well to stop."

Reprieved. But I was disappointed in myself and in them for not being disappointed.

I didn't tell them what Sitt Miriam had said to me. She herself wrote to them soon after, alluding regretfully to a certain lack of progress.

I never found out anything further about Nur's rooster.

Dancing

We were driving around and around in Beirut, my father and I. He had come down, as he did every so often, to go to a meeting or to buy things we couldn't buy in our little hill village. He did what needed doing efficiently and alone, because if he brought Mother she might dillydally or become engrossed in talking to someone. Before he drove home, he usually checked in with Fräulein, our matron at school, just to see that everything was going as it should with the four of us.

Today, though, he'd stopped in at school and picked me up to come along. There were no bundles in the car to show he'd done errands, and yet here we were just driving around. This was so out of the ordinary that I didn't know what to think.

It was December and drizzling, so Father had snapped the curtains into the car windows. The isinglass, cracked and foggy, shut us into a very small space together. I looked over at him. He was wearing his second-best fedora, the one with the stained band, and a white shirt, unstarched and frayed around the collar. The rest was gray: narrow knit tie, unmatched jacket and pants, even his socks. Under his jacket he had on the gray wool cardigan Mother had knit him. His shoes, black, were the ones made by the village cobbler who understood bunions. They had an extra large rounded part over the big toe of each foot.

Father looked the way he always did for weekday business in Beirut, except his eyes were fixed ahead, his jaw tight, a cheek muscle jumping. Traffic was heavy around the Government Center, especially in the rain, so it took a lot of attention, but I didn't think that was it. I saw that he had his pulpit look, the one that said, *This is serious, Margaret.* I'd heard my friends' parents call him the conscience of the mission. *He looks like the con-*

science of the world, I thought. I waited. Nervously.

Finally he cleared his throat, and took his eyes off the road a minute to look over at me.

"I want to talk to you about dancing, Margaret."

I gulped without meaning to. I made myself wait some more.

"I think it's time we discuss it, so you can think about it and make a decision."

I was almost fourteen. Social dancing had just burst on me as the preferred way to spend every waking minute. My theme song, the words and music that ran through my head continuously these days, was: *Heaven, I'm in heaven, and my heart beats so that I can scarcely speak. And I think I've found the happiness I seek, when we're out together dancing cheek to cheek.* Then there was "Smoke Gets in Your Eyes," "Tea for Two," and "Making Whoopie." I knew all the words.

I didn't think this was the time to tell him all that. But I said, "Father, I love dancing. Some of the older boys have begun to teach me how and I practice, so I know several steps. We have about twelve records we play on the Victrola."

I noticed that my father was keeping an even tone. "Fräulein says you dance over the noon hour, in the afternoon, and after supper. If that's true, when do you get to your homework? And when do you play outside?"

I brushed that off. "I do my homework. I play outside. Don't worry."

My father ran his finger around the inside of his collar. "Do you know what I refer to as Arab dancing? The *debke,* for instance? Belly dancing? The women in scant clothing?"

"Yes."

"Do you know I don't approve of that dancing?"

"Yes." Long pause. I was thinking that belly dancing, the *debke,* and scant clothing have nothing to do with how we dance at school, nor what we wear. But I knew this was no time to point that out.

A car horn blared impatiently behind us. Father sucked in

his breath and jerked forward. Still he held on to his level tone when he spoke again.

"Margaret, do you see how inconsistent it would look to our Syrian friends for my daughter to dance when I disapprove of their dancing and have told them so?"

I was beginning to feel locked in. I pulled over as far from him as I could and started drawing on the steamy passenger window.

My father turned to look at me and narrowly missed a bicycle. The rider swerved and yelled, "Sheepherder!"

My father said, "Then there's another part of it. The fact is, Margaret, that people can get quite—well, excited—when they dance. It's having their bodies close together like that."

Had he ever danced then? Had this excitement ever happened to him?

He said, "I never danced till I went to college. When I got there, I was older than most of the other students, you know, because I'd worked for a while first. I had to work there, too, so I didn't have much spare time or spare money. A friend of mine told me he thought I ought to loosen up, to learn to enjoy myself. He suggested we go to a church dance, and he would introduce me to a nice girl. Against my better judgment I went."

"Did you dance?" I asked. "What did you think?"

"I danced about five minutes," my father said. "I couldn't go on."

"Oh, but it's easy," I said, knowing fully we were on two different tracks, but going on anyway, as though I didn't. "You just have to stick to it and listen to the rhythm."

"No, I got too aroused. I knew it would never be right for me to dance."

We drove for a while in silence, he thinking, I'm sure, that he'd warned me about Danger Out There, and that now I would fall into line.

I had never felt sorry for my father before. Well, I had felt sad for him; this was more. For anyone to discover that he mustn't, couldn't, should never dance seemed a terrible deprivation. I didn't understand it. I saw that he felt ashamed. I would never have expected him to feel ashamed about anything. He was always so proud and so right. The shame seemed to be connected with getting excited. It was shameful to get excited. That was it.

I felt excited too when I danced and my heart beat so that I could scarcely speak. But I didn't feel any shame, only intense joy. I felt ashamed and guilty about lots of things lots of times, but I felt none now. My father's shame seemed to have nothing to do with me.

I knew what my decision was: *YES, YES, YES to dancing. Dancing was the loveliest thing in the world.*

I turned to my father. "I've made my decision. I don't need time to think about it. I am going to dance."

The sun glowed through the isinglass.

My father drove me back to school in silence.

That wasn't the end of it. Neither my father nor I would give in. I continued to dance; he continued to check with Fräulein. He would deliver another lecture. And another.

I experienced it as sunshine and rain. I danced and I was scolded. I danced on.

What I Did This Summer

It all began with the *National Geographic*. Up until I discovered the issues with African tribeswomen and native boys, Sundays had been very boring. Every Sunday of the school year, my brothers and I walked from boarding school in West Beirut to church in the American compound downtown. Then, since our parents were in Souk-el-Gharb and Grandma considered us motherless chicks, she always had us stay for dinner afterward. At the end of the big Sunday dinner, Grandpa and Grandma faded away in naps down the hall, while the three of us went to the parlor to read, preferably something uplifting. No games and no noise.

I was fourteen that spring. Where I wanted to be was at the Roxy Theater matinee, seeing Sylvia Sidney and Henry Fonda in "The Trail of the Lonesome Pine," or Douglas Fairbanks, Jr., in anything. In our family a movie would have been unheard of for a Sunday afternoon, so there I was in Grandpa and Grandma's parlor. Lined up behind glass doors in the parlor bookshelves, I found every *Geographic* right up to the last month's issue, May 1936. I made a secret index of the more uplifting ones. Sundays were better after that.

Later that spring, in the parlor, I found something more: a whole book of Greek statues, page after page of naked bodies. Except for fig leaves on some of the men's things, they were right there for me to look and look. After I grew used to the marble bodies, I began comparing their heads to the horses' heads in the chariot races. They had the same stretched look, no soft roundness anywhere. Because the marble was white, I imagined the men as white-skinned and golden-haired. I took the book out on Sundays, whenever I had the parlor to myself. I called it my "research."

I could have taken the book back to school to show my best friend Leah, but I didn't want to share it. At least, not then.

Madame's class was the last one, and she said what she always said just before summer vacation: "Have a happy holiday, but don't forget all your French. Read the books I have assigned to each of you, and write me a small essay in French called 'What I Did This Summer'—with beautiful grammar."

My brothers were already at the car and waiting. Father asked Arthur to carry my trunk down the stairs and up onto the baggage rack. Arthur grumbled some, but he went. Last of all, he and Philip roped their bicycles on top, and then we were ready to go. Everyone was sweating by then, but especially Father, impatient at how long it took to get anywhere, and nervous about driving the mountain road to Souk after dark.

Just as we were pulling out, Leah ran over from the playground waving her arms. I risked Father's boiling anger, and asked him if we could wait a minute. Leah panted up to the car window and pushed her head toward me.

"You forgot these," she said and handed me the summer reading books I'd left behind in Madame's class.

"Oh, thanks," I said, wondering how she could be so dumb, but not saying anything that might bring on one of Father's sermons.

"Ask your folks about coming up to Shemlan soon," I said to her, "and I'll walk over from Souk."

"I'll write you," Leah said.

Once out of Beirut, we cooled off. Past the orange groves and the sandy stretches of date and banana palms, we started the hairpin turns up the mountain road. The terraced vineyards began and olive trees; with each turn we could look down and see Beirut wavering in its muggy air. I felt jubilant. What a good word.

The jubilance lasted about a week. I always forgot how the long free time turned into long empty time. Oh, there were things to do—reading all I wanted, drawing, picking fresh flowers every day and arranging them for the house. Any time I felt like it I could go to Im Najeeb's, just over the stone wall. I'd sit on the floor next to where she always sat, her legs tucked under her black skirt. From there she leaned forward to steer cloth, with smooth authority, through the portable sewing machine that said "Singer" in gold curlicues across its front.

This time when she first saw me, she said how I had grown since last summer and how my hair was as soft as a cat's. She looked at my small starting breasts and laughed while she patted her own big ones and said, *"'Sm Allah! 'Sm Allah!"* She took measurements for my new green-flowered dress, and scissored with her fingers in a wide circle around my chest to show how she would cut out the cloth to leave me growing room.

Then she ignored me while she fitted her customers, and they whispered about blood and deformed babies and bad men in the village. Sometimes I wanted to ask questions, but I didn't speak so that the women would go on talking, thinking I was either deaf or grown up enough to hear.

About the third week, the exciting stories at Im Najeeb's began to be less exciting with no one to share them. My brothers were all right, but they were always starting wrestling matches or some other boys' stuff, and my little sister, Anna, wanted to play dolls all the time or have me tell her about boarding school. I realized I was missing Leah.

Leah and I were used to each other. We liked doing the same things—drawing, or making up a play and acting it out, or dressing up. If we were just sitting around she'd ask me what I wanted to do and then we'd do it—except for playing tricks on people. I might think up a trick on a teacher or one of the kids we didn't like, but she'd usually feel sorry for the person before the trick got done, so it was no fun. She was much too serious that way.

One thing I liked about her—she didn't hold a grudge. Take the time our sixth grade put on "Treasure Island" for the rest of the school. I was Jim Hawkins and Leah was Long John Silver, with her right leg strapped up behind her under a long black cloak. Her leg really did look amputated. She used a forked stick for a crutch, and the audience gasped when she came on. That was the scene where she and the other pirates sat around on the ground singing, "Fifteen men on a dead man's chest." As Jim Hawkins, I watched from behind a cardboard rock. The scene was a hit, but when Long John Silver continued to sit there after everyone else was off, the audience began to titter. The thing was, Leah couldn't get up by herself with just one leg, and I was laughing too hard to go back onstage and help.

Finally I did. But all that afternoon Leah wouldn't look at me or speak to me. By the next day though, when our class talked about how the play had gone, I noticed Leah laughed with the rest of us about that part.

Even though I'd known Leah longer than anyone, I didn't tell her about that research I'd been doing. She asked me sometimes what it was like to have brothers, but I always pretended I didn't know what she meant. The fact was, it didn't help any to have brothers. Everything was so private at our house.

Once, I walked into my parents' room in the middle of the day and found my father taking a sponge bath at the washstand. The folding screen was pushed aside and he was naked, bent over the porcelain basin, washing his armpits. He must have just come up from the garden. His sweaty clothes lay on the floor at his feet, fresh clothes on the brass double bed. I saw all that in a second, along with his stunned face—stunned that I had come in the door and had seen him. I saw his brown face and hands, the rest of him white, as white as those marble statues. But where there might have been a fig leaf, I was too frightened to look. I rushed down the hall to the stairs and out to the garden. My father never spoke of it to me, and although he must have told my mother, she didn't say anything either. I'd never told Leah about that.

I missed her, especially after a month and a half had gone by. So I was excited when I got her letter:

"Everyone has gone to the mountains. They say Beirut is

worse than usual this summer. . . ." I skipped on: " . . . so we'll be at Melcone's *pension* as usual. See if you can get permission to come for a week. Mummy says Sarah can sleep on a rollaway cot in their room and you can share my room with me. We can talk all night. Sarah is jealous, so we have to be nice to her if we're to be allowed to do this." She ended with, "We'll have such a good time!"

Mother gave her permission right away, though we'd still have to ask Father, of course. She said, "Maybe Im Najeeb could get the green dress done in time, so you'd have something new to wear." Then she looked at my hair and tugged at some of the extra-short places.

"Father really did hack it off this time, didn't he?"

I started to get tears in my eyes, angry all over again about my latest haircut and how there wouldn't be time for it to grow out before I went to Shemlan.

But then my mother said, "I'll see if I can get a message to Jurius. Maybe he could give you a trim just to even it. We can afford that, I think."

I understood from that that Mother would pay for it if Father wouldn't. Every once in a while, for something she thought mattered, she would go to her private bank account. I loved her for knowing how much this mattered.

Jurius, the barber, was our cook's son. He had his shop in Shemlan where he cut the hair of most of the summering missionaries. His own black hair was oiled smooth like Cesar Romero's in a poster outside the Roxy, and his white starched coat smelled of the perfume he put on people's hair when he was done. My father had his hair cut there for special occasions, but he didn't let Jurius sprinkle on any perfume. Father said we couldn't afford Jurius. He'd ordered a barber's kit from Montgomery Ward and cut our hair himself.

That afternoon, while Father was behind his study door practicing his sermon, Jurius came to our house to visit his mother. He cut my hair in the cook's room off the kitchen, and finished it off with a healthy splash of perfume.

Father looked over at me at supper. "Say, Margaret, I did a pretty good job this time, I think. Not bad for a home haircut. Wouldn't you agree, dear?" He looked across at Mother, who had told him after this last one that she thought I was getting too old for home haircuts.

Mother chose that good-humored moment to tell him about my invitation to visit Leah. Sometimes he would think of the most unexpected reasons for me not to have fun. This time he said, "I don't see why you shouldn't accept." Then he spoiled it by bringing up my table manners and a tendency to forget to thank my hosts for a good time.

I was very meek and the moment passed. I suppose they knew they had nothing to worry about, nothing about morals, since Leah's parents were missionaries too.

There would be no card playing or dancing, no evils like that.

Now with my hair looking better and my new dress all hemmed, I focused my attention ahead to seven whole days of pleasure, to eating meals in the big, cool dining room at Melcone's and to the time I would have with Leah. I would have to watch my table manners, remember to say thank you, and resist needling Sarah, but that was a small price to pay.

I thought I knew exactly what to expect, but the second day, in the dining room at lunch, the unexpected happened. We were having *bettanjan mashi*, my favorite stew of lamb and eggplant, but I stopped eating when a new family followed the head waiter in. He led them to the most desirable table, overlooking the terrace with a view of Beirut harbor. There were four of them, father and mother and two sons. The sons wore neat tight-belted, gray flannels like Douglas Fairbanks, Jr., instead of the baggy corduroy knickers I was used to seeing.

The taller of the sons strolled elegantly to the table and sat with his back to me. He was probably a head taller than I and, I guessed, two years older, sixteen. His hair was fair, almost white, in short curls close to his head. He didn't look like anyone I knew, but I felt a shock of recognition. After he sat down, he turned around in his chair and surveyed the room slowly. When his eyes met mine, I saw they were an intense blue.

"Nathan," I heard his father call him. Nathan.

Leah whispered, "Hey, aren't you done?" We excused ourselves from the table.

Outside on the terrace, Leah said, "Come on, let's go. Are you asleep or something?"

We got to the pine grove. "You be *la belle dame* first," I said. "I'll be the knight-at-arms. Here I am over here, alone and palely loitering. Do I look pale enough? How should I do loitering?"

Leah made up a fairy song to sing as she rode my pacing steed, sitting side-saddle on a fallen pine. In the dry, rocky field beyond the grove were wild daisies, and I made a garland of them for her hair. Leah's face got all dreamy as she sang and rode.

Being the knight let me be with Nathan inside my head without Leah's knowing it. When the time came for her to lull me to sleep on the cold hillside, I closed my eyes and let myself imagine what our first words might be.

"Where have you been all my life?" seemed perfect, but he looked so sophisticated, I thought *when the chance does come to speak I may just look at him and be altogether dumb.*

I waited for the dinner gong, waited to see him. But when we walked into the dining room, I found I could look at his table only if Nathan were looking away.

Leah's mother said, "Margaret, are you feeling all right? You haven't eaten a bit of your soup and now it's all cold."

I made myself pay attention to our own table and put Nathan out of my mind, but my eyes wandered over there again. The mother was pale with dark hair and dark eyes that looked intently at nothing. Nathan's father hovered over her, urging her, "Eat, Meena, eat. Just try to eat something." Then a minute later, "Try some of this good soup of mine, Meena. You'll like it."

She seemed not to hear him, or anyone else, and soon she

left the dining room, walking stiffly and slowly as though each step needed to be thought out. I watched her leave and when I looked toward Nathan, his eyes were on me.

Leah and I left and played Parcheesi in our room. I felt like hugging the world, and I even said, "What about letting Sarah play with us?" Of course, she stayed too long, and we had to get in bed so she'd leave.

After we were in our beds with mosquito nets all tucked in, with only the light from the sky outside our window, Leah said in a slow careful voice, "Do you want to get to know that new boy? What do you think he's like?"

That was the moment when I could have said something like *I think I'm under a spell.* But I'd feel silly. It was easier to say, "Let's just see what happens. We don't have to go out of our way."

After I said it I felt relieved. Leah seemed relieved too and changed the subject. "Have you started your essay for Madame yet?"

How typical of Leah to start something for school this early, I thought. How different from me. And how different she was about Nathan. As my true friend, why didn't she feel the same way I did? Well, she didn't, but I shouldn't have to tell her what I was feeling. She should just know.

I said, "I'll probably do what I always do—write it the day before school starts."

On the third day after Nathan arrived, I went to our room, expecting to find Leah. The room was empty, and I was about to go look somewhere else when I heard Leah's voice coming from the next room through the open window.

She was saying, "... it's that she acts so sort of bored, as if she doesn't want to be here." Then a minute later ". . . I don't understand what's wrong with her."

I squeezed in tight to the window wall, listening. Leah's mother said, "Well, I've always thought Margaret was quite moody. I've said that to you. And self-centered. Just ignore her."

Silence. Then her mother tried again, whispering this time,

"Maybe she's just having her period, dear."

I heard a sniff, then a nose-blowing, and Leah said very low, "I don't think that's it. I think I'm boring. I think she gets bored with me and then tries to be nice."

I tiptoed over to my bed and lay down to read in case she came in. I had never known her to cry, but from the sound of her voice that might be next. I didn't want her to cry.

I promised myself I would pay attention to our play, not let myself get distracted. We spent the next day on our costumes. A royal blue *abba*, worn backwards and belted with a silver *lamé* sash, made a fine damsel's gown. We slipped the sash lower on Leah's left hip like the illustrations in the book. Her mother loaned us a white silk shawl for a veil under the crown of daisies.

The knight-at-arms' costume wasn't as easy. My red skirt worked for a cloak, but armor was a problem. Mr. Melcone found us some heavy cardboard cartons to cut into breastplate and shield. The oatmeal color wasn't right, but we didn't have the patience to paint them and wait for them to dry.

Leah was so pleased with her costume that she kept checking to see if I wanted to trade. We went back out to the pine grove for a dress rehearsal.

When Nathan and his brother came out to the tennis court to use the backboard, I kept my eyes sternly away, turning my back, and mentally plugging my ears to the sounds of the ball and their shouts to each other. I hoped if I didn't look at Nathan he wouldn't see me. When their father came out they began a game, Nathan against the two of them. I wanted to watch and cheer.

So far we had exchanged no words, nothing but looks. I was beginning to think that was all there would ever be.

Now it was the evening of the fourth day, the end of the supper hour. Chairs scraped back as families left their tables to walk outside on the terrace. Young Arab waiters in white jackets and slicked-down hair swarmed in to clear up and sweep under the tables. The adults stood around talking, except for Nathan's mother, whom I saw walk silently back toward their room.

We children, nine of us, drifted together into the warm darkness, back toward the terraced vineyards behind the *pension*. I had put on my new dress with the green flowers. I felt new, too, and glad about my haircut.

Everyone looked at Nathan and waited. "We could play Sardines," he said. I admired his cool voice, a voice that seemed to say: *I merely suggest it. I know a million magic things to do.*

No one had heard of the game; not I, certainly. The others all shook their heads. Even Walt, who must have played this game before, deferred to Nathan.

"Well, here's what you do," said Nathan. "One person is It and that one goes and hides while the others count."

One of the bolder boys said, "Sounds like plain old Hide-and-Seek to me."

Nathan ignored the interruption. "The one who's It can hide anywhere outside. The others count to one hundred and then go and look." He paused to see that we were all paying attention. "This is the part that's different. When the others find the one who's It, they hide with him and stay very quiet, instead of yelling or running in to home base. Got it?"

"So then we're all packed in tight like sardines," I said, getting it. "Yeah, let's play that."

When Nathan was It, I was the first to find him (or rather, pass by him in the stone shed where he was hiding). I felt him grab me around the waist from behind and pull me to the back corner all in one motion. It was very dark in there. The dirt floor gave off a smell of dampness and sheep's wool and manure. My heart thudded in my eardrums so loudly, I was afraid Nathan could hear it. To quiet it, I crossed my arms over the hard little lumps of my breasts.

After a while I tried to speak. Nothing came. I felt him trembling all along the side of my body, heard him breathe as though he'd been running. Then I felt his hand, gentle and dry, touch my face, across my forehead, over my eyes, over my cheekbone to my ear, smoothing over my hair to the clipped back of my neck.

"Soft . . . so soft," he said.

I held my breath. His hand came lightly down the front of me, stopping to circle first the closest breast, then the other, with one finger, slowly. I let out a gasp of shock and joy. His hand made a dive for mine and we held on to each other's hands.

I heard someone stumbling through the weeds outside the shed. "Blast!" said Nathan.

"Darn it," I said agreeing, but lying too because I felt relief at the same time.

With three players, then four and five, and then eight packed in, giggling and shushing each other, it became the greatest game in the world. We took turns keeping watch through a chink in the wall when anyone came close.

We took a count and realized we were all there, all but Leah, and there were no more sounds of searching. I thought of Leah out there alone, humiliated probably, and too proud to call out to us. I thought of calling, "Here we are!" But the moment passed.

Sarah began to tell "The Pit and the Pendulum." Back when I was ten like her, that was the scariest story I knew. But I was done with that now. We listened for a while, then one by one we began to stretch and to complain about being squeezed or poked in the eye. The game was over and nothing else qualified. Sarah's voice trailed off.

I heard the players' mothers call them in for bed. There was no one calling me. For the first time in my life I could probably stay up all night. Nathan kept looking over at me. When the others were gone, he walked over closer and took my hand.

We walked back and forth on the big main balcony and leaned over the balustrade to pinch and sniff leaves of lemon verbena, growing in gasoline tins along the edge. The stars were out. I found Cassiopeia's Chair, my upside-down initial in the sky, as I always did. Far below we could see strings and clusters of lights that were Beirut and beyond them the shimmer of the sea.

It was all right to be quiet. I thought, *I will always remember this night, holding Nathan's hand, being all alone with him.*

Nathan said, "I want to tell you something I've never told anyone."

I waited, every part of me listening.

"I don't believe in God," Nathan said.

I stopped walking and reached out for the railing. I had never known anyone who didn't believe in God or in Allah. I was afraid to even think what might happen to Nathan. In Grandpa's *Illustrated Bible,* the sky split open when God spoke, and powerful white rays blasted down to earth. The child Samuel in the Temple listened as the rays came down. God cast Adam and Eve out of the Garden of Eden. Lot's wife looked back, crying. God turned her into salt. That's what God could do. There were no pictures of anyone not believing in God.

Nothing happened. No thunder, no lightning. The constellations kept their places, unchanged, in the sky.

Nathan went on talking and walking, so I had to catch up to hear what else he was saying. *Perhaps he doesn't mean it,* I thought.

"My older brother, Maurice—two months ago he got sick. Then he got really sick. The doctor said it was typhoid, but he knew Maurice had a strong constitution and he'd be all right. He got sicker and we all prayed. I made a bargain with God, that I'd believe in him and do whatever he said, if he'd just let Maurice live."

He stopped talking and I saw him swallow hard. I waited, not knowing what else to do. Finally I whispered, "What happened then?"

"He died. God didn't keep his end of the bargain, or maybe He never made a bargain. But here's what I think. There isn't any God up there at all, so all this praying to Him and talking about Him is rot, just rot." Nathan's voice sounded high then, like a girl's. He collapsed onto the stone floor and began to cry, rocking, and hitting his fists on the stone. He shuddered to a stop, then began again.

I knelt down on the stone floor next to him and gathered myself around him. We stayed huddled like that for a long time and he got quieter. A question came to me and I was almost afraid to ask it, but I had to know. "Is Meena—I mean your mother—is she sick too?"

Nathan looked at me a moment, confused. The moon was up and I saw him look at it and then back at me with eyes all puffed up from crying. Then he said, "Oh, you mean because she doesn't eat or talk to anyone, sort of as if she's asleep? She's been like that ever since Maurice died." He began to talk about Maurice, how smart he was in school, how handsome, how the girls were always trooping after him, how brave he was. He was funny, he told wonderful jokes. "I think my mother loved him the most," he said and cried again.

We were both so tired. Finally I think Nathan was just out of tears. We lurched to our feet and hugged each other goodnight. I went up to Leah's and my room. Just before I opened the door, I heard the light switch off. I undressed in the dark and fumbled around to get under the mosquito netting and under the sheet.

"Leah?" I said.

She didn't answer.

I tried again. "Leah, can you understand about Nathan and me? I never felt this way before."

The silence went on so long I almost gave up. Then Leah's voice came out of the dark, sounding as if she had a severe cold. "You forgot all about me out there, didn't you? Just the way you forgot me in 'Treasure Island' and left me on the stage so people laughed."

I started to say, "But you laughed, too, afterward. I thought it was all right."

Leah kept right on, heavily, like some stone-footed giant in a nightmare, nothing stopping her. "What kind of friend are you, Margaret, if you can forget me so easily when something else comes along?"

I said, "Leah, I didn't . . ."

She talked right through me. "I just figured out that we've known each other six years, ever since that day your mother brought you into my first-grade class to visit a real school. Do you remember that? She was teaching you at home. You're my oldest friend."

I thought, *I've known Nathan four days but I think about him every second.*

I knew I owed it to Leah to acknowledge what she'd said and tell her I knew how I'd hurt her. I tried to. There seemed to be a boulder sitting on my chest. I could hear in Leah's voice that she had been crying, probably for quite a while. I wished I could cry. I thought it might help the pain in my chest.

The next morning Leah lay without moving in the next bed. Quietly, so as not to have to talk to her, or risk having her want to come too, I pulled on my clothes from the night before and went to find Nathan.

The balcony was still puddled in places and broom-striped in others from the early morning sweeping. Someone had watered the lemon verbena plants already; their gasoline cans overflowed, their smell filled the air. I went over and stood in the spot where Nathan had cried and I had held him.

From there I looked through the glass doors of the lobby and saw Mr. Melcone tidying up his front desk. I went in, pulled a chair over next to him and then just sat there.

He smiled at me, a good-morning smile that used his whole face and his mustache. "You are looking for Nathan perhaps? His family hired a taxi very early for Beirut. They hope to get a booking on this afternoon's boat back to Haifa."

Mr. Melcone wasn't your usual grownup. He looked at me, stopped smiling, and then reached into the mail slots behind him. He pulled out a small piece of lined paper, folded several times and glued shut. "He left this for you."

Dear Margaret,
Sorry not to see you today to say good-bye. My father was waiting up for me when I got in last night. He

wasn't too pleased. Then he said we have to go back home to Haifa. We came because of Maurice's death, but now my mother doesn't want to be here with all these strangers. I wish I could stay. I told my father that, but he said we all have to be together, especially now. I guess he's right. I was pretty soppy last night. Sorry. Don't forget me. Write to me. I think I love you.

    Nathan

I read and reread my letter, folding it and putting it in my pocket for the pleasure of opening it again and pretending it was the first time. This was a true love letter, the first I'd ever had.

When Leah woke up, I was there waiting to go to breakfast with her. I didn't tell her anything. Leah was silent and looked straight ahead as we walked. I knew I should say more about last night, but I just couldn't.

After we were in the dining room, Mr. Melcone made a kind of general announcement that the Lewis family had asked him to say good-bye, since they had left so suddenly.

Please don't say anything about Maurice or call it The Tragic Loss. Please don't.

He didn't. That was all.

I felt rather than saw Leah give me a questioning look. I shrugged ignorance.

In the two days before I went home, it seemed at any moment as though Leah might speak about the strangeness between us. Half of me wanted her to, so I could say Nathan's name, show his letter, live it all again. The other half of me dreaded any more talk. That half kept seeing Leah stumbling around in the weeds in the dark, while I hid with Nathan and the others.

I went home. I felt as though I'd been away a long time. My mother said it was good to have me back and that she'd missed having my fresh flowers in the house all week. My father smiled at me and then reminded me I must write to Leah's parents and thank them. I said I would.

I noticed that the dull feeling in my chest wasn't going away. What had started as pain that night in Shemlan was still with me. It seemed to get sharper now when I pushed my sister Anna out of my room, when I told a lie, or when I remembered my French books not even opened to the first page.

I worked a secret hour on French, enough to know I could do it when the time came. I even liked *Cyrano de Bergerac* from my brief dip into it, and felt a surge of fondness for Madame, who had given me a sparkling glance along with the book and said: *"C'est un livre bien romantique. Tu vas l'aimer."*

I didn't love it. That would be going too far. Still my chest felt a little better. I ran through a few sentences to put into my French essay, "What I Did This Summer." "I visited my friend Leah and her family in Shemlan. I made some new friends. You could say nothing much happened."

I didn't answer Nathan's letter. At first it was enough just to have a private coziness I could reach into whenever I felt ho-hum or lonesome. *Nathan loves me,* I would say inwardly, and it always worked. There was endless time to write back.

After a while I began trying out letters in my head. When I pictured the Nathan whose cool voice told us how to play Sardines, I began:

> Dear Nathan,
> How are you? Things have been quite boring since you left. I'll be going back to school soon, so at least I'll be with my friends, but . . .

When I pictured the Nathan who cried, I wrote:

> Dear Nathan,
> I'm sorry about Maurice dying. I don't know anyone who's died, and I don't know what to do that would help. I want to make everything all right. You're so brave not to believe in God. No one has ever said I love you to me. I'm glad you love me. I love you too.

•

I thought about Leah. Even though I would be seeing her at school in a month, a letter to her began to write itself in my head:

> Dear Leah,
> You were right when you said I forgot about you when Nathan was there. I did and I'm sorry. I know I didn't tell you what was happening with me, but I thought I shouldn't have to tell you. I expected you to be a mind-reader, I guess, when really, I should have told you what was important to me. Maybe this will sound funny to you, but he looked like some Greek statues I saw in a book at Grandpa and Grandma's. I'll show them to you some time. He told me something he hadn't told anyone else, and he wrote that he loved me.
> Your friend,
> Margaret

I sealed it and found a stamp.

• Part Two •

Furlough Year, 1937:
In Pursuit of the Worthwhile

We sailed from Beirut on a July afternoon, 1937, heading for Naples. My parents and my younger sister, Anna, could be said to be going on furlough, since they would be away for a year; but it was to be much longer for me. I was going to America to finish high school and go to college, as my older brothers had done. It was unthinkable that I might never come back, but I was too excited about going to think about what I was leaving. My best friend and neighbors from Souk-el-Gharb were at the dock to see me off, but I hardly noticed them as they hugged and kissed me good-bye. The S.S. *Esperia* blew her departure whistle; loudspeakers warned non-passengers in English, French and Arabic to disembark; slowly vibrating, she began to move out. In the hills above Beirut, I saw flashes of light as the sun reflected on friends' pocket mirrors, flashes that said *Good-bye*. I pulled out my mirror to signal back.

My father had spent all year planning for this month we were to have in Europe on the way. Somehow, he had to make it financially manageable, stretching his missionary salary to its limit. Frugality would be essential, but my sister and I, eleven and fifteen that summer, must squeeze out of it every bit of culture we could. True to form, Mother took no part in the planning, content with whatever father might choose to include or leave out. He was to be the sole guide in this pursuit of the worthwhile.

When we docked in Haifa that first afternoon, I complained to him that I wanted us to be on our way, not hanging around here in what seemed like a second Beirut. He pulled out a rolled-up package and gave it to me. It was one of those pink paper-bound composition books the French call *cahiers*. Ours had Jeanne d'Arc on horseback on the front and we used them for compositions in school.

"I bought this for you, Margaret. Use it as a journal of the trip. If you're restless you could start now. And keep it up every day so you don't forget anything."

Though the *cahier* bore the taint of school, I began to write in it the next day. The adorable sailor, who stood at the top of the gangplank when we came on board in Beirut and again at Haifa, gave me long, soft looks and remembered my name after he first heard it. Writing about him stretched out the pleasure of those minutes. No danger I'd ever forget him. I kept the *cahier* under my pillow.

Naples: "I had to say good-bye to the sailor. He called me 'Magurite' and squeezed my hand, while he looked at me with a speaking look. I wish I were Italian."

Pompeii: "I am startled that it's so small. I expected something grandiose, more beautiful, cultured, etc. But it just seems sort of squeezed and pathetic—narrow streets, small rooms. It was awfully interesting though."

Rome: ". . . So many uniforms gallivanting around." I described the ones I admired most, then listed St. Peter's, the Church of St. John Lateran, and the catacombs. (Father might read my *cahier*.) "We took a bus out to see a great arena for athletic events commissioned by Mussolini, where we saw *Il Duce* and *Viva il Duce* and once *Dux Credere, Obsidere, Combattere* painted on the walls." I was proud I could figure out what they meant. "I wish we were staying longer." But we went on to Florence.

Father had talked about Florence. He still remembered the name of the *pension* on the Arno where he had stayed twenty years ago on the way to Lebanon, and he had written months in advance for reservations.

When our train from Rome reached the outskirts of Florence, Father looked over his stack of used envelopes for his penciled notes and itinerary. There were certain paintings we must look at carefully at the Uffizi gallery and the Pitti Palace:

all the Botticellis, Guido Reni's *Mary Magdalene*, a portrait of Peter in tears after he'd heard the cock crow the third time. Was that by Rembrandt perhaps? Father wasn't sure. We would see the *David* in the square. There were lots of imitators and lots of copies, but none of them came near Michelangelo's *David*. And we had to see his unfinished pieces.

"Wait till you see them, Margaret. It's as though live people were struggling to free themselves from the stone they're caught in."

Back home near Souk I had found clay in the hillside and had modeled the heads of a man and a woman. After that Father seemed to consider me a sculptor. Now he turned to me to share his feelings about Michelangelo. Even though Mother and Anna were sitting right there with us on the train, he looked at me when he talked, seeing me as the artist of the family. Often when we saw sunsets he would ask, "Is that puce, would you say, Margaret, that part over there? And magenta, perhaps?"

I'd feel flustered, but I loved his asking. There, on the train, I wanted to take his hand and promise to walk through every gallery, to look at every view, to go to every spot he remembered.

The museums were crowded and airless, but we stayed for most of one day and came back the next. Together we looked at *Mary Magdalene* with her auburn hair and sad, guilty face. I bought a print of the painting in the museum shop, carrying it rolled for the whole trip (and leaving it behind on the last train). It was hard to move away from the Botticellis with their dreamy, innocent faces, hair like light clouds, and filmy draped bodies. Father had recommended them; now with me he got embarrassed and nudged me along. When we came to Saint Peter, though, we stopped a long time and I saw he had tears in his eyes. Anna and my mother sat down to wait outside where there was a breeze and where Mother could rest her bad knee. For those hours I was my father's and he was mine.

Father remembered a small jewelry store on the Ponte

Vecchio. He had us wait outside till he came back with three small packages: a mosaic pin for each of us, black ovals inset with wildflowers. Each was different and each was beautiful. Gifts from him were rare and momentous.

Every minute was filled in from Father's list of worthwhile sights. At first if a museum or cathedral was closed, I would suggest a movie I'd seen advertised. Father would have none of that. Instead he went down his mental list, or checked the guidebook for some other museum, gallery, or great person's home. It was useless to suggest alternatives.

When museum admissions were more than Father had budgeted for, he would sigh and pay, scowling. Once while we were sitting in a park, an attendant told us there was a charge for sitting there.

My father countered angrily, "How dare you collect money from people sitting in a park? Parks should be free. In America parks are free." Later, sighing heavily, he went over his column of expenses once more.

We took the train to Venice, to Milan, to Geneva, always taking bags of bread, cheese, and plums to eat on board. A routine emerged. At each of our stops, we heaved our collection of suitcases and bags of food through the train window to be watched over by Anna and Mother. Then I stayed with the luggage while the others went with Father to find out how to reach our hotel by bus or street car. If our lodgings weren't on a main line, Father would question taxi drivers until he found one whose prices seemed manageable. Then he would stow Mother and Anna in the taxi to wait, while he went back for the luggage and me.

I didn't mind the carrying itself. Doing it made me feel strong and essential to the family, but it did interfere at times with my private life and with the private game I played. It had no name, nor did I allude to it in the *cahier*. This was the way it went: We would board a train and there would be a boy. Quick exploratory glances, longer looks, then a delicious brush past each other in the train corridor, a shoulder touch while we stood between cars, waiting for the lurch that would bring us to near embrace. No words. Once, though, a boy next to me at the train window went through a recitation, possibly his whole English repertoire, to a conveniently-placed stranger on the siding. Thus the boy let me know he knew English, thought I was nice, and would like to make friends. Tunnels were an exciting bonus, being fitful and of uncertain duration.

Then we would come to our station. I would get off, watching to see if the boy got off too, but even if he did, the game was over. I had to stay with our pile of bags and then, a suitcase in each hand, shove and push my way after Father, already almost out of sight ahead of me. By the time I was halfway through the station my ribbed cotton stockings would start to bag. My mother insisted I wear them, but my garters were weak. If I ignored them, the stockings crept steadily down around my ankles. I'd stop and give them a quick yank up, then clutch my suitcases again before Father got out of sight. With all that, there was no time to look for the wonderful boy. I suffered until the next player showed up.

Other Americans, a different breed from us, strolled through the station with one or even two redcaps carrying their matched luggage. I watched them pay, casually, easily, with smiles and thank-yous. We never hired redcaps and used taxis only when absolutely necessary. Father would ask how much, then finger down into his limp coin purse and pay, examining each coin to be sure he had it right. He included no tip, since he felt overcharged already. Our driver would take his money and mutter, or give us all a look. I would feel deeply ashamed and hold it against Father.

We went to Switzerland and then to Bavaria, to see the Passion Play produced every ten years by the townspeople of Oberammergau. Walking through that town was like tiptoeing down the aisle in church, so contagious was my father's awe.

Father had counted on seeing the play, had even put the money aside for tickets. But it appeared there was no play that year. Surely there was some mistake? He asked in French, German and English. No, no mistake. Instead he had to be satisfied with studying the large black-and-white photographs of the principal players from years past: Jesus of course, Judas, Mary. He scrutinized those pictures whenever we walked by them. If he could, he would have taken a part in the passion play—not Jesus', I think, but Peter's.

I wondered how it would be to take the part of Judas. Would the townspeople shun you while the play went on and afterwards?

"Oh, surely not," my mother said. "It's just a play after all, not real life."

Father made an indignant face.

She said, "Of course, I know, it's a very important play, dear, but still. . . ."

I had my own yearning in Oberammergau. I'd saved most of my allowance (a Syrian pound a month) and I wanted to spend it on something memorable. We looked in every shop. I narrowed down the looking to a certain size and to a certain animal—a fawn—not a Swiss bear, or a cow, or an Alpine cottage, or a scene from the pageant. Those would have cost more money than I had and I didn't want them. My fawn waited for me to spot him, displayed on a blue cloth with a few other carvings on the sidewalk. The carver stood nearby with his arms folded across his chest. His asking price was exactly what I had. I bought it. My father stayed with me for the entire search and never said, "Wouldn't this one do, Margaret?" about any of the fifty fawns we'd passed over. He smiled at me when I took the package.

When we reached Munich late the next night, we found all the cheaper hotels and *pensions* filled because of a guild festival in progress. Our taxi driver brought us to the house of a friend who could put us up, if we would take what he had—one small bedroom with a double bed and a loveseat. One of us could sleep on the feather comforter on the floor. We had been on the train all day; we accepted the room with relief. I pushed the red velvet loveseat to the window and looked down the street, draped in long colored banners, a different color for each guild.

Three blocks away a great crowd had gathered, clapping and yelling after each sentence spoken, or rather screamed, by a man on the platform. When our host came to see that we had everything we needed, he gestured out the window. "Everything is good now for Germany since the Leader has come," he said. *"Wunderbar, wunderbar."*

In the night I heard the heavy feet and male voices of Hitler Youth, singing in cadence as they marched under our window. Some of them looked my age and they seemed very handsome, but I could not imagine playing the game with even the blondest, most beautiful one. I had already noticed that German and Swiss boys didn't give the long, soft looks Italians did. These Hitler Youth never glanced to either side, but looked intently forward, like crusaders pursuing the Holy Grail. I felt disappointed.

We went to Mainz and took a steamer down the Rhine to Koblenz. On the trip, instead of having us eat our usual provisions, Father ordered lunch and then a bottle of Rhine wine with four glasses. Even my mother was startled. He wanted to be romantic and celebratory, and we all felt the excitement and smiled at each other, taking our first sip. The wine was very sour, but Father didn't return it. Perhaps he felt too ignorant about how the wine should taste to risk doing that. No one drank any more, though it was unheard of to waste anything.

Years later, when my father and I were talking about drinking and he listed the evils of drink, I reminded him of the wine he'd ordered on the Rhine, hoping to hear him say there were times when drinking was all right.

He said huffily that he might have known he would be called to account for that. "You see what happens, Margaret, when one makes exceptions, breaks the rules. Nothing but bad comes of it."

I wanted to say, *But I'm not calling you to account—just the opposite!* I had loved his gesture, but he had already judged himself and didn't want to talk about it.

We took a train to Cologne, then Paris.

I had been constipated for a week. I ate the skins from my plums and everyone else's, drank huge mugs of hot coffee and hot water, sat patiently but with increased anxiety, trying every morning. I felt heavy, barely able to walk. At the Louvre we mounted the wide marble steps to the second floor, where the *Winged Victory* stood. I had looked forward to seeing it, but all I could do was take a glance and make my way to a stone bench. From there I went to another bench and then to another, careful to sit on the edge.

My mother, who would give an enema even when someone's disposition needed improvement, saw that this was not a question of disposition. She sent Father off to buy an enema bag. Several hours passed. When he got back he triumphantly displayed the result of his quest—a small red rubber syringe called a *poire*. It was cheap and he'd learned a new French word.

Mother and I took over the bedroom and left Anna and Father to the couches in the small second room. When it was done, I lay on the double bed and slept. No enema for my disposition had ever left me feeling so blissfully light, relieved, and grateful. When Mother came to bed we talked, as it seems to me now, all night.

She told me that when she and my father married, he had never kissed a woman before. "I come to you clean," was what he said to her on their wedding night. She told me she had fallen in love with someone else and had expected to marry him; when he told her he would have to go back to America to break off his present engagement, she'd sent him away instantly. I didn't understand why she'd done that, but I did understand that she'd married Father with different feelings from those she had toward that other man.

I told her my most intimate, my most deeply held secret, about Nathan and the summer before. My mother was thirty-six when I was born so she was fifty-one then. Hard to believe. That night she seemed like a wonderful older sister.

I revived after my ordeal with the *poire*. We returned to the Louvre, climbed the Eiffel Tower, saw Notre Dame, and even the World's Fair and the Russian exhibit.

We took a channel steamer and went on to London, our last stop. We saw the Tower and the Abbey, Buckingham Palace and Madame Tussaud's Waxworks. Down a dark, little back stairway an arrow pointed to the "Chamber of Horrors." There would be an extra charge so Father refused to go, Anna was afraid, and Mother's knee hurt. I went on my own, doing something I wanted to do and, blessedly, by myself. I walked around the show slowly in tingling excitement. Then I went around again.

We had visited eleven major cities and they were beginning to run together in my mind. I was tired of sleeping in tiny, hot rooms on lumpy beds or couches, and never understanding the language. I was tired of feeling my father's anxiety and irritation. By the end of that month, I knew how much I disliked Father's watchfulness to be sure I was taking in all that I should. And I was tired of being with the family all the time, trudging to the next museum. If only I could have walked alone through the park, any park, in the rain, gone to the Folies Bergéres, taken a gondola instead of the motor launch through the Venetian canals. But at least there'd been the "Chamber of Horrors."

My last entries in the pink *cahier* were brief, hardly more than lists, but I'd kept my promise to write. I packed the journal away.

America

We sailed to New York from Bremen, this time on a German ship. I flirted with the sailors, but they weren't as ready to play as the Italian sailors had been. They seemed stiffer, and busier, more grown up.

Of the last furlough I remembered very little; the incantation of our address—87 Sherman Street, Hartford, Connecticut; being eight years old; learning to rollerskate; lumpy plateaus of darning on the knees of my ribbed stockings; forgetting my Arabic and later having to learn it all over again.

Now as we sailed into New York harbor I thought, *This time I will remember everything.* There was the Statue of Liberty, looking exactly as I imagined her. I felt like crying with no idea why. I saw tears in my father's eyes, from pride about being an American and pleasure about being home. For me, and surely for Mother, Lebanon was home, but this was certainly exciting.

After we landed, a customs officer noticed the silver stickpin Father had made by cutting out the head of Liberty from a dime. When my father responded with pride that he had made it, the officer told him it was against the law to deface American money. For the first time I saw my father being treated without deference; I even thought for a horrified moment he might be arrested. Father took the stickpin off and poked it in his pocket with a look of shame, like a criminal.

In the hot tedium of the customs lines, I looked and smelled and listened: more freckles than I'd ever seen, red hair, light skin, blue eyes, almost all English words to be heard, but with so many variations—some that I couldn't even understand; some black and some oriental faces—I had never seen their like before.

Outside the dock buildings: the roar of traffic and car horns, smells of hot dogs and hamburgers, French fries and popcorn, great billboards advertising cigarettes, liquor, Coca-Cola, and skyscrapers that blocked out the sun.

My father bought a second-hand car and learned to use a clutch and gear shift. In traffic he was likely to forget how and the motor would die. "I've killed my engine," he would say in the exaggerated accents of a yokel to cover his embarrassment. He would sweat and start the engine jerkily. We drove to Wooster, Ohio. Away from big-city traffic Father did better and remembered to put in the clutch when he shifted.

We moved into a small frame house in a row of identical houses reserved for missionaries on furlough. There were three bedrooms on the second floor. The one Anna and I shared held our twin beds and a desk I could use for doing my homework, Father said. The other two bedrooms were a little larger, one for my parents, one for my brothers, who had transferred from their colleges to Wooster for the year. Downstairs was a dining room, a front living room and a good-sized kitchen. The furniture came with the house and, like the house, was practical and shabby. Even pots and pans and dishes were supplied. A large Philco radio stood at one end of the dining room. We listened to "Amos and Andy," "Jack Armstrong" and "One Man's Family."

Mother had never run a washer and said it was beyond her. Father had never used one before either, but he did all the laundry, using the wringer washer in the dirt cellar. Shelves covered with cobwebs and grit waited for the jars of applesauce we would put up, and bins for potatoes and onions.

The back yard had rough weeds and a place to hang the wash. Several trees gave us their small, wormy apples that were free and made good applesauce. My brothers played catch there.

I started eleventh grade. Classes were large, forty or so in a room instead of the four I was used to at the Community School in Beirut, and we moved to each new class—English, civics,

Outside our house in Wooster, Ohio
Furlough year, 1937

math, biology, French. The first few weeks I kept getting lost, then I got used to finding my locker in the hall, got used to the noise, the rush, and the jostling between bells. Except for civics, nothing was new, so I did no homework and coasted. In homeroom between classes, I watched the girl in the seat ahead of me fish out a pocket mirror, balance it in front of her on the desk, and comb her fine long hair until every hair was in place. Then she would peer critically at her reflection and dab powder on her nose. She was my ideal of sophistication.

The boy behind me knew the words of most popular hits and murmured them—"Deep Purple," "The Lamp is Low," "Blues in the Night." He asked me if I liked Claude Thornhill. When I said, "Who's Claude Thornhill?" he didn't speak to me again. One or two girls smiled at me after class.

At noon I walked the mile and a half home, swallowed some lunch and then hurried back. Anna would be home for lunch, and, of course, Mother. I didn't say much to them, but it was comforting and familiar to be with them for a little while. Once a week Mrs. Almstutz came from her farmhouse in the Amish community to clean and iron. She was efficient and strong, and had a calming effect on Mother, who often seemed over-whelmed. She and Mother would sit over coffee at the kitchen table, Mrs. Almstutz stirring her cup and making little mounds of bread crumbs, while she told stories about her children and the animals on the farm. She was a large woman with a plain face and complicated sentence structure. Anna and I experi-mented stringing words together the Almstutz way.

Sometimes after school I walked part of the way with Nancy Miller (one of the girls who smiled at me), if she was going to her grandfather's chiropractic office. In October, after we'd been in school a month, she asked me if I liked to dance. A boy in our class had asked her to invite me to a Hallowe'en dance at a classmate's house. I had been secretly looking at the boy and hoping, since the opening day of school. He was very attractive, I thought, but mute. When I was near him, I was too. I knew Nancy must have engineered this and wished he'd asked me himself, but I was pleased, sure this was my opening step into a new world. Nancy planned to go. Could I? I was sure I could. We walked slowly, planning what to wear, and imagining how it would be.

I told my mother about the invitation the moment I got in the house. She seemed pleased for me but she didn't discuss the question of what I could possibly wear with the passionate interest I wanted from her. I decided she was just tired, and I waited for my father to come home to give me permission.

He came home. He went upstairs to the bathroom. Finally he came down and went out to the kitchen, where my mother was peeling potatoes at the sink. She was using a peeler and he told her why a knife was better—faster and less wasteful.

I tried to summon the tone I'd used telling my mother about the invitation. I hesitated, my words stumbling as they came out.

Mother said, "Margaret's been invited to a party. Nancy just invited her, that nice girl she walks back from school with sometimes."

"What kind of a party?" Father asked, made suspicious perhaps by her soothing presentation. He turned to me and asked again.

Mother began to murmur that I would be with Nancy, though the party wasn't at Nancy's house.

"A dance party," I said and waited.

"Then you don't go." His answer was absolute.

"But why not?" I asked. "You said you didn't want me to dance while we were in Lebanon because people wouldn't understand. But now we're in America."

My father was unshakable. "Not while you're under my roof, Margaret."

It was the end of the world. To be asked in, to be almost there, and then have Father say no and slam the door.

Yet I still felt some hope because I knew my mother felt differently. I looked over at her.

She said in a faraway voice, "Don't you think it would be all

right, Will? We could telephone the family. . . ." her voice
dwindled. She too saw it was useless. I felt doubly wounded. I
might have expected it from him, but from her?

I cried and cried, but I didn't argue. I didn't talk to him at
all for several days. During that time I thought about how to get
through the year, and particularly how to deal with him.

One way to block him out, and block out my angry feelings
as well, was to read. I stopped at the public library on my way
home from school, walked down the aisles, pulling down books
until I couldn't carry any more. I took them up to my room or
to the back yard and once started, I was oblivious. My brothers
were tolerant about it; they had their own lives and spent most
of their days and nights at the college. Anna missed me, and my
reading frustrated her to the point of tears. Mother soothed her
and accepted my reading as she accepted most things we did.
"It's just a stage she's going through, dear." My father was
pleased that I was reading. Sometimes he made a gesture as
though to check what the books were; usually he seemed to believe that if the covers were worn and came from the public library, they must be all right.

The second way I found to block out my father was to go to
the movies. I began to go to matinees whenever the movies
changed, several times a week. Nancy showed me how to slip
into the theater free about twenty minutes after the feature began. We whispered explanations of the part we'd missed. If the
usher caught us without tickets and raised a fuss, we went to a
different theater for a while.

Since we ate an early supper, everyone would be halfway
through by the time I got home and slid into my seat. I would
start on my bowl of tepid soup while family conversation fal-
tered. Father would begin to interrogate me. The questions
were always the same. Where had I been? What movie did I see?
Why had I gone? He would tell me I was not to go again. The
next time the movie changed I went.

One rainy afternoon in January I went with Nancy to a
movie with Greta Garbo and Charles Boyer. In one scene

Charles Boyer, as Napoleon, stood in front of an enormous wall map of Europe, with his shadow falling on it just where his conquests were to be. I nudged Nancy to be sure she caught the symbolism. If I wasn't in love with movies already, I fell in love then.

When we came out, it was darker than usual and we realized the movie had run for an extra hour. Meanwhile the rain had turned to sleet. The streets and sidewalks were glassy, trees and bushes encased in ice. Nancy suggested we telephone my house from her grandfather's office. We slid there, holding hands.

My calm reaction to Father's anger over the past months was all an act. I knew I was pushing the limits. I both expected and feared the moment when he would say, "No farther, that's enough." This might be that moment.

He answered the phone. His voice was neutral, not the blast I was expecting. I heard him say to my mother. "It's Margaret. She's all right." He listened as I told him where I was. A minute of consultation, then he came back and said Arthur would come for me in the car. It was too treacherous underfoot to walk home.

I waited. Then Arthur came and pulled into the chiropractor's parking place. As he drove me home, he told me that everyone, even Philip, had been frightened at my not showing up. Father had been sure when the phone rang that it was either the police or the hospital. Arthur was his usual collected self, not worried, merely reporting all this to me.

To my surprise, Father stopped battling me about coming home late for supper. I continued to go to after-school movies, but less often. It didn't seem as important.

Then I changed my name for him. Up to then he was always Father, though once when I was younger, in a moment of closeness, and envious of Leah's calling her father Daddy, I had asked if I might call him Daddy. "Absolutely not," he said. "Father is the name for fathers to be called. The name Daddy is baby talk."

"Dad, then?" I said.

"Father," he said.

This time I didn't ask his permission; I simply began calling him Pappy. I arrived at the name by a private route. I noticed that he sucked his teeth to get rid of food while he was still at the table, and that he cleaned out his ear wax with a pencil. He tucked his napkin in his collar when he ate his soup, and he made eating and swallowing noises. I couldn't comment on any of these things directly, but I looked on them and him with disgust, deciding he was hopelessly primitive. His most serious offense was trying to control me and breaking what I considered a promise that I could dance in America. My backlog of rancor produced Pappy. At least I knew how to deal with him—stand back and laugh. And wait for him to go back to Lebanon. He accepted Pappy without comment.

As for Mother, I thought it didn't matter if she stayed or left. She disappointed me. It seemed a long time since that night in the Paris hotel.

As spring came, I began to notice some of the boys my age who lived in the row of houses on our street. We went for walks around Miller Pond and in the woods on Saturday afternoons, reading poetry aloud, talking about the theory of evolution, and whether there was an afterlife. Sometimes we kissed. When one of the boys came to my house in the evening, we would be awarded the living room without even having to ask. At ten o'clock my father would come in and start winding the clock on the mantelpiece. That was all he did; the boy would go home. Once I accepted a date with a boy in my class who was generally agreed to be Bad, but he was boring and his breath was awful. I dropped him.

I started to write for the school literary magazine, got a part in a school play, and began to sing in the chorus.

I saw that my life hadn't been ruined after all when I'd missed that Hallowe'en dance party. The shy, attractive boy had dropped out of view, but I didn't miss him.

School ended. Our lease on the little house ran out. My

brothers each found a summer job back in their college towns and we said good-bye to each other. Father and Mother and Anna packed up their trunks. I moved my things to a missionary dormitory where I would live my senior year at Wooster High. Meanwhile I was to work and help out on an uncle's farm until school began. Father and Mother and Anna dropped me off on their way to board their ship in New York.

I hardly felt like the same person I had been a year ago. I felt American, tough and knowing about boys, about God, about anything you could mention.

My father said, "In seven years when we come back you will have finished college, maybe married, maybe even have a child." He looked at me seriously. I didn't answer. I wouldn't let what he said have any impact.

I turned to my mother. How small she had grown this year; when I put my arms around her I felt her thin shoulders. I had stopped looking at her or talking to her as the year had gone along. There was a brief twinge in my heart, but I pulled away.

"Good-bye," I said and started to wave.

Precious Jewels

My brother on the phone, long distance, "Mogs? It's Philip."

"Yes," I said. "Oh, God. Is it Mother?"

"She's had another heart attack. Rachel and I put her in the hospital last night and she's holding her own, but I'm calling to see if you can come down."

I had a picture of my mother lost in a starchy hospital bed. In pain? Unconscious, hooked up to tubes?

Philip's voice broke in. "What do you think, Mogs? Can you get away? You thought you couldn't when Father died . . ."

"Are you telling me she's going to die? You said she was holding her own. And don't call me Mogs." I stopped myself. "Sorry, Philip. Of course. I'll take the first plane out of Logan. I'll call from New York when I change planes."

I felt mechanized, a robot. No time now for the tune running in my head, some long ago hymn. I'd pay attention to it later.

So call the university and leave a message for Bill if he's teaching. Call Northwest about the next Boston–New York flight and a connecting flight to Louisville. Arrange for the children to go next door after school. Cancel the dentist. The most important thing—talking to the children about their grandmother—I'd have to leave to Bill for now.

An hour later I walked outside to watch for the airport limo. I thought of Mother on her last visit, three months ago, and of our talk about heart attacks and dying.

In the kitchen over coffee, I had asked her how she was doing, meaning, how was she doing without Father.

"I *miss* him," my mother said. "Not a day goes by when I don't think of him and miss him."

I waited for her to go on, with the numbness I always felt when I thought of Father. I had not mourned him at his death or any time in the two years since. Any sadness I felt now was for my mother's loss, not mine.

Mother said, "You know, all those years in Lebanon, your father kept himself so busy with mission work I never seemed to see anything of him. He drove himself so. Then when we retired and went to Louisville, I thought, now we'll have some peaceful time together." She sighed. "He really couldn't rest, be peaceful. He didn't have the faintest idea how to do that. And then he died."

I refilled our mugs—Mother liked hers scalding. Over the rim she looked at me through misted bifocals.

"When I die, I know I'll be with him. That's a comfort to me."

I looked away, probably found a few crumbs under my chair to pick up. Touchy subjects, both of them—my father and the afterlife. Better to leave them both alone. Mother didn't foist her beliefs on me, or say she prayed for me anymore.

When I listened again, my mother was telling me about what her new doctor had said, mimicking his accent: "Now, Ma'am, I don't want you fretting over what I have to tell you, but your heart has gotten a bit tired here lately. That last attack just kind of wore it out some. But you're not to fret yourself, you hear?"

She was hardly fretting.

Shocked, I said, "But why were you so pleased to find that out? That worries *me* a lot."

My mother patted my hand. "Don't you see? This way I know I'll just go off, and not hang around being a burden and nuisance to everyone. That's the only part I've ever worried about, and now that won't happen. I never was afraid of death itself."

I couldn't go on with this. I said, "We really need to get going to the grocery store, okay?"

She stood up with a small wince. Arthritis. She was probably

Mother

five feet tall. I remembered when I reached her height at fifteen and could stand eye-to-eye. She'd shrunk, I thought, even since she was here last.

At the kitchen door Mother turned to me. "I have to say, sometimes I think I don't ever want to die: when I see something that takes my breath away, like the sky when the light is going, or a spider web after the rain, or a *zinzilacht* when it's first in bloom. Do you remember our *zinzilacht* trees in Souk, Margaret?"

I said, "I think I can smell them."

Then we'd gone out to the car and shopped and stayed clear of troublesome subjects.

Traffic on Route 2 was heavy, the tunnel clogged to a standstill for minutes at a time. I looked at the back of the cabdriver's head and made myself unclench my hands. I could take a later shuttle if I had to.

The limousine put on a burst of speed at Logan and dropped me abruptly under the "Flights Boarding" sign. Once aboard, I breathed deeply and let my mind go where it wanted.

I imagined Mother here with me on the plane. She'd flown for the first time when she was sixty, and now she, who was always timorous in a car, couldn't get enough of planes. She especially liked eating on planes, because she thought the airlines' packaging ingenious and the food delicious. And always for her there were the people. If she were with me now and I turned back to my book, Mother would be talking to someone within minutes. Someone she'd never seen before would be pouring out a heart-rending life story while my mother nodded and made listening noises. If there was time, Mother would give her life story in return.

When she wasn't talking to someone she'd be people-watching, making up mini soap operas about them, like: "Did you see that little girl who just came down the aisle with her mother? Did you notice the expression on her face? That's from foot pain, poor little mite. She coaxed her mother into buying her those pointy, pink shoes with the little heels. And now her toes hurt and she doesn't dare say a word or her mother will say, 'You know what I said.'"

I would laugh and make up a scenario too.

When the family teased her about her addiction to soap operas, she acknowledged it and went on watching. Once she said to me, "Sometimes I can smell the ether when I watch 'General Hospital.' I was such a good O.R. nurse. I loved the challenge of handing the right instrument to the surgeon smartly with no fumbling, no matter how he barked at me. The surgeons are much nicer on 'General Hospital' than they are in real life."

When I saw my mother, I wanted to tell her how it was when we were sick as children. She could tell if we were running a temperature by kissing our foreheads, though she would get out the alcohol-bitter thermometer too. I admired the way she shook it down and then how serious and professional she'd look when she read it. She knew when bedrest was called for and when it was safely over. Later, with my own children, I thought I should know all that to be a proper mother, just like her.

The plane roared into La Guardia. I pushed my way off and found an empty phone booth.

My sister-in-law, Rachel, answered. "Your mama's resting peacefully. She's in Jesus' hands. You just keep on coming, and don't worry. Philip will be there to meet you at the airport. See you soon, honey."

I boarded the plane for Louisville, feeling relieved, even exhilarated. Rachel was wonderfully reassuring. Even her inevitable introduction of Jesus seemed only mildly irritating, since I was focusing on Mother. Two more hours and I would see her. The plane took off. I closed my eyes.

The airline hostess came down the aisle with her clattering cart of beverages, but I kept my eyes shut and the cart moved on.

I slept and saw a family photograph taken in our garden in Zahleh. There is Mother and next to her Father, sitting on straight wooden chairs brought out from the house. Anna is a baby in her lap, my brothers and I sit on small chairs in front. We are all smiling for the camera, but Mother's smile is not posed. She is looking down at Anna, thoroughly enchanted. She seems sure of herself, content. Were you, Mother?

Out of my half-dream I could hear my mother answering me, "That was the happiest time in my life, when you children were small and all around me."

We were all around her but not my father. Zahleh neighbors would shake their heads over how hard it must be to have him away so much. Looking back, I think it wasn't hard, though she never let anyone know.

As I got older I saw that while she wanted more laughter from him, he wanted more (he'd probably say) moral fiber from her. When he was away she was light-hearted, dropping everything to go for a picnic, reading to us for hours at a time, playing checkers past mealtime and bedtime.

My father probably thought, when he married my mother, that at twenty-eight she was more serious than she was. She was serious about her work as a nurse, but not much else. She loved to laugh. She wore pretty clothes when she wasn't on duty. Nurses all wore starched white uniforms to the floor then, and starched caps. She was proud of hers, but she knew she was dashing in red. Then she married Father. He held views about clothing: it should be modest, sturdy, and cheap. He did buy her one red dress. He had to go to Turkey on mission business. When he came back after half a year away he brought her a red Kurdish dress, hand-dyed, hand-woven cotton with fine green embroidery on all the seams and down the front and sleeves. She wore it on furlough when she gave mission talks.

My mother told me once that when Father asked her to marry him, she knew she didn't love him. She told him so. But she thought he'd be a good father. She did come to love him, and he gave her four children. That was how she put it.

I remember a day when I was nine, about to go off to boarding school in Beirut. My mother and I had been sewing

Father brought these clothes from Mardeen, Turkey,
to wear for missionary talks.

name tags on my black ribbed stockings and long underwear, and I was telling her again how I hated having to wear them. "How do you know I'd get cold without them? I just don't get cold much."

I remember we sat on her brass double bed with the white seersucker bedspread. Serious almost to tears, she said she had something wonderful and holy to tell me. And then she told me about menstruation.

At the end she said, "When *that* happens to you, you'll be a woman and, just think, you'll be able to have babies with someone you love."

That last caught and amazed me. When would all this happen? "We don't know," she said. "It could be next week, next year. Not the babies, of course, but the other."

I couldn't wait to announce that something wonderful was going to happen to me. I made the announcement at supper that night. I said we didn't know when—it would be any time now. Anna, who must have been five, wanted to know what the big secret was, pouting at my being the privileged one.

I wouldn't tell any more because it was our secret, my mother's and mine, but it seemed I'd already told too much. After supper she took me aside and said I must understand we didn't talk about that, especially not in front of boys and men. Arthur had gotten a funny look, she said. I felt ashamed but didn't know why. She hadn't said there was anything wrong about it.

That was when she told me how when she was fifteen, living in that mission house in Tripoli, she'd waked up one morning and found herself lying in blood. She rushed out to the courtyard screaming that something terrible had happened, while her five younger brothers and sisters looked on with open mouths. Habooba, the younger ones' nursemaid, hustled her off and told her she wasn't dying. She was humiliated. Grandma had never given her one word of warning.

So she wanted it to be better for me. I had my first period the summer I was fifteen, six years after she'd prepared me for it. By that time I'd given up hope of its ever happening, so I didn't know whether to believe the little rusty spots on my underpants. If this was it, I felt cheated. I called my mother upstairs in a tentative voice.

She put her arms around me and said, "Now you're a woman, dear."

She looked at me, waiting for me to say it was wonderful, but all I felt was embarrassed.

I was even more embarrassed when she told Im Najeeb over the stone wall. Im Najeeb came back with pads she'd made out of her dressmaker scraps. I remember hissing to them both that I knew where to buy proper pads in Beirut and that was what I was going to do. Mother soothed me and thanked Im Najeeb and said we'd buy pads in Beirut.

How impossible I was. She'd told me about herself at fifteen, about her panic and shame, and to make sure I didn't go through anything like that, prepared me years in advance. All I saw at the time was that she was awkward at it, using words that were idealizing and romantic. I needed to get to her and tell her what I now knew, that she had done it out of love in the best way she could. Another hour to go.

The wisp of hymn tune I'd been hearing since morning grew clearer, accompanied by some long-forgotten words, "Precious jewels, precious jewels. . . ." My mother singing, the words and tune wavering up and down as though blown on a light breeze. I lay with my seat back, my eyes closed, and went deep and still, to catch the soft sounds.

I was in my white iron crib in the first house, the mission manse in Zahleh. My brothers lay in their beds across the room under the high windows. We'd heard "There were ninety and nine in the fold that night," Arthur's choice. And Philip's—was it "Shall we gather at the river?" Now it was my turn. My mother let down the side of my crib so she could sit close. Her dark hair was coiled in a figure eight on top of her head, with tendrils that curled at her neck. She drew me up to sitting, and I smelled her familiar smell, like vanilla. Her left arm went around me. Her cheekbone rested on the top of my head as she sang.

"Precious jewels, precious jewels . . ." and something about a crown. I looked out to the night sky beyond our stone wall and saw royal blue and purple, the color of the jewels. I was a jewel, I knew, the only girl after two boys, a jewel.

My mother sometimes called me Precious and My Precious when I was little. They were her names for me alone.

"When he cometh. . . ." The second verse. "When he cometh. . . ." Oh, then he would make things better and straighten out things, whatever they were. That was when Father and God, interchangeably, were in charge of the world.

I had a melting sensation, as though under a gentle beneficent rain, and all was well.

A long-ago never-confessed sin. Would I have a chance to tell her now?

Mother, you know those thick obstetrical volumes you thought were safely hidden in the dark trunk room? I never told you, but all one summer I read and reread the part about home delivery: ". . . if possible, see that the bed is raised six inches with blocks of wood . . . stack newspapers and then soft sterilized cloths on the bed to soak up the blood." "What to do if the expectant woman has a bowel movement during delivery." Was that really a possibility? I decided not to have any babies, at home or anywhere else. If I'd told you, you would have put it in perspective, but I was too guilty to tell you then. So I'm telling you now. Silly, isn't it, but you understand.

Now I was thinking about a harder thing to tell her. It was about the furlough year, when we lived together in the little missionary house in Wooster. At fifteen, I was making discoveries every day. One was about evolution. I was amazed. Another, and just as amazing, was that I needn't be afraid of Father anymore.

Until then, I'd always felt close to my mother, and pitied her for the life she led with my father. I thought I needed to defend her. But as I diminished him, I began wondering why she didn't defend herself, show me that a woman could fight when she needed to, didn't have to get silent or teary. To punish her for that and for not having a checking account and for not learning to drive and for not even learning to use the washing machine, I stopped talking to her and ignored her instead.

She never asked me what was wrong and I never told her. When the furlough ended and they went back to Lebanon, I told myself I was glad to be rid of them both. Now I could get on with my life and start using dark nail polish.

I was never aware of missing them. I kept my distance. For seven years, till their next furlough, I'd write now and then, not about anything that mattered. Mother's letters would ask why they hadn't heard from me. From 1938 to 1945. They wrote that it must be because of wartime censorship. If my mother guessed that I was angry and wanted to be distant, she never said so.

By the time my mother and father came back to the States, I'd graduated from college, married Bill, and had my first child. We never talked about that year in Wooster. It simply receded. But I remembered it now—an amputation I had performed on myself and pretended was nothing.

I felt the plane start its descent. My mother's presence began to fade as the plane landed and taxied to a halt.

Bless Philip! I spotted him immediately, grayer, heavier, so his cotton jacket pulled around the armholes. He hugged me and called me Mogs. I let it pass.

In the car I realized after a few miles that he was driving toward his suburb, instead of going through the city to the hospital. "We'll go get Rachel first," he said.

Rachel opened the door and enfolded me in flower-scented rayon. Over her shoulder I saw the two of us and a smaller Philip multiplied over and over in surrounding mirrors behind swag lamps and turquoise loops of drapery. Rachel offered iced tea, a bath, a nap, after the long trip. I felt impatient.

"Can't we just go over to the hospital now? I really want to see her," I said.

Philip looked away.

Rachel came up and put her arms around me.

"She's gone, dear. Blessed Jesus took her this morning after Philip called you."

I stared at them. All that talk about Jesus had fooled me entirely.

"Do you mean to say she was already dead when I talked to you from New York? That you said what you did, knowing I'd think she was still alive?" Out of breath, I plunged into tears.

Philip and Rachel cried with me, Rachel amply, Philip wiping the corners of his eyes with his fingers.

"She seemed to slip away between one sentence and the next," Rachel said. "One minute I'd told her you were coming, told her again because she couldn't seem to keep it in her mind, and the next minute she was gone."

Philip said, "Last night when we took her to the hospital, she asked the doctor if she could still visit you in New England as she'd planned. He told her, sure, if she'd rest well. She was so pleased about that. Told me what he'd said several times after he'd gone."

I cried again. She'd gotten what she wanted—to just go off and not hang around. But I wasn't ready for her to go. I was like an undersea diver, all tangled in seaweed and tentacles of love and anger, regret and disappointment.

There were all the things I'd wanted to tell her: that it was none of my business how she was with Father, that I regretted terribly the years when I'd rejected her, that she'd been a good mother.

I telephoned Bill and the children. Our oldest understood the finality the most clearly and began to tell me what he would miss: Grandma's reading "Rikki-Tiki-Tavi" to him and listening while he practiced the flute. Our daughter said, "You mean she isn't going to come this summer and sleep in my room with me? She always gave me a back rub to help me go to sleep. She said nurses do that." Our youngest wasn't sure he remembered her but he reacted to tears in my voice and said he didn't want me to cry.

A month later, back at home, I had this dream:

I was in a huge empty coliseum. There were no seats. There were millions of small file drawers, tier after tier of them all around, each drawer with a white name tag on it. I knew this was where all the people of the world went when they died. I started on a long flight of stairs that began in the center of the coliseum and went up out of sight. When I got halfway up I met my mother coming down. Her hands were full of bracelets and brooches and necklaces which she laid in my hands. Then, in a measured, ceremonial way, she put a long amethyst necklace around my neck.

I said, "I'm going up. Come with me."

She gave me a long steady look. Then she said, "No. I have to go over there," and she pointed past my shoulder to the files for the dead.

I awoke and took the time to gather in the dream and make it my own.

I thought of my mother's cameo and her Florentine pin, gifts from my father, her gold wedding band, the blue sapphire ring, the crystal necklace. Anna and I had decided what to do with each one. But there was no amethyst necklace among them.

I thought about it.

Then I remembered once again the hymn she used to sing to me—"Precious Jewels." I was special and precious to her, and so I was special and precious. In the dream she put a royal necklace around my neck, a gift to wear forever.

Father

Every story about my childhood seems to end up being about my father. He takes over, as he did in life.

Now I'm saying to his ghost, "If you keep on interrupting I suppose I'll have to pay attention. I will go back to your beginnings, bring back all that I know about you and guess at the rest. I will recall our whole history together, not just the anger, then maybe . . ."

So this is the story of my father.

The curled sepia photograph says "Willie, Age 8, Springfield, Illinois." Feet together, hands to his sides, dark eyes ahead. It could be titled, "Life is real, life is earnest." He seemed to know already that nothing would be easy and nothing free.

The oldest of eight children, he was named William after his father, the silent stranger who worked six days a week in the local watch factory to buy food for the table and make payments on the house at 1226 North Third Street. Nothing easy or free for him.

When Willie was eight, his mother told him it was time he got a job. A woman up the street, who made doughnuts at home, hired him to deliver them to her customers on an early morning route. He chose to start off before breakfast, even though he was always ravenous. By the time he came back, his mother had a fire going in the cook stove and had packed her husband's lunch bucket, ready for him as he ran to catch the tram. Willie would have his mother to himself in the warm kitchen, after his father was gone and before the others were up.

One morning, after he had delivered the first few orders, a heavy snow began. He kept going but his head started to feel cold and wet. He reached up, realized his cap was gone, and, looking back saw nothing but his own disappearing footsteps. Shivering, he thought of his mother spooning a clunk of hot hominy into his bowl. He hid the undelivered doughnuts under someone's porch and ran home.

His mother opened the back door when she heard him stamping off snow. "Why Willie, how quick you were this morning!"

He basked in her smile and her treat—a dab of butter on his hominy. She hung up his jacket to dry near the stove and then said, "Willie, where's your cap?"

At eight, in this household, one didn't lose things. "Some big boys came along and took it, Mama." He kept his eyes down on his bowl. He felt his face get hot. He looked up and she was looking at him. He never forgot her look.

"And the doughnuts, Willie?" she said.

He put on his wet jacket and went out again, slowly, hoping she would call him back. He retraced his route and delivered the doughnuts.

His cap never showed up and he had to wear a scarf around his head for the rest of the winter. The other children poked fun at him and asked him if he was a girl, but that was nothing compared to how he felt about the only lie he ever told his mother.

Father told me that story with biblical solemnity. Hearing it, I saw my grandmother-in-America as a fountain of goodness, like a giant stone figure in a park. Or rather in his life. Father didn't need to explain to me the lessons of that morning: always finish what you start, never let someone down who is counting on you, don't waste anything or lose anything, and don't lie to your mother or to anyone else.

Some time in high school, at a church service with his mother, Willie pledged his life to God's service. I have a picture in my mind of how that came about.

Father

On Sunday mornings he polished his boots and his mother's shoes. She brushed his jacket, made over from an old one of his father's, and they walked to the United Brethren Church on the corner. Willie's father stayed at home. Sometimes the other children went along, but more often it would be just him and his mother.

One Sunday, a guest preacher came to town and from the pulpit whispered and shouted about pledging one's life to Jesus. Willie held himself still beside his mother on the hard pew, while his heart drummed heavily and his body seemed about to fly apart. Then he felt himself catapulted toward the altar.

After he'd made his pledge and turned back from the altar, he could hardly believe it was still Sunday morning, still Springfield. He walked back down the aisle, and saw his mother's eyes on him and tears on her cheeks. From then on his mother called him Will.

In his heart he wanted to be a doctor, had wanted that as long as he could remember, but he knew better than to waste time wishing for the impossible. His pledge to Jesus brought him a scholarship to a small church college in Tennessee and then to a seminary in Chicago. He worked at whatever part-time jobs he could find around the college and did the same at theological school, saving every nickel, never spending money on foolishness. When he could afford to, he'd go home to Springfield to visit his mother. He wrote to her every Sunday. He did that as long as she lived.

At the end of his time at the seminary, the Presbyterian Board of Foreign Missions offered him a three-year appointment in Syria, what is now Lebanon. No one in his family had ever left the United States. The idea of being the first was both heady and unnerving. He would have to learn to speak Arabic, not just read and translate it, as he did Latin, Greek, and biblical Hebrew. The whole venture would be a test of his faith, but he voiced his doubts to his mother cautiously.

His mother had no such doubts. She wrote back: "You're doing what the dear Lord told you to. You know that." Then she added: "I pray every night, dear boy, that your doubts will fade away like the morning mist. Take them to the Lord in prayer, as the hymn says."

He stopped questioning then, lest he risk seeing that look on her face when he'd lied to her, age eight. Having serious doubts now would mean he had lied when he went to the altar. He accepted the board's offer to go to Syria.

Once there, he was asked to be principal of the Protestant Girls' School in Souk-el-Gharb in the hills above Beirut. He lived at the school, taught all day and spent his spare time studying Arabic. He told me he used to take long walks between the hill towns, carrying flash cards of Arabic vocabulary, saying the words aloud as he walked.

Older missionaries in Beirut noticed this serious, intent young man, approved of him, and invited him down for tea and for Sunday dinners after church. He never admitted he was lonely, but he accepted the invitations, walking from Souk two hours down, three hours back, grateful to be asked, though he always felt ill at ease. He never had known how to make light talk, never had a sense of fitting in.

He met my mother at a tea at the Jessups'. Being invited to the home of the first missionaries to Syria was a special privilege. Their house stood imposingly in the mission compound, shaded by royal palms. Inside the door, he flicked road dust off his boots, grateful he'd remembered his handkerchief. In his eagerness he had walked fast and was sweating profusely. He wiped his face and neck. That done, he tiptoed across thin oriental rugs to examine tapestries and paintings of Arab scenes. What he saw seemed opulent after his bare room at the Girls' School and, before that, at home in Springfield, where everything was bought for its practical use and wearing qualities.

No one else had arrived. The Jessups greeted him, standing together at one end of the long parlor, Mrs. Jessup genteel, Doctor Jessup kindly, with a white mane. Will watched while Mrs. Jessup and a maid in an apron crackly as butcher paper carried in a brass samovar of tea and trays of cucumber sandwiches.

Doctor Jessup asked him something in high Arabic. After a struggle, Will translated in his mind and answered in Arabic that his lessons were coming along. He wondered what to say next, but before he could think of anything wise and grammatically correct, Doctor Jessup moved toward the door, where other members of the mission community were starting to arrive. He breathed again and edged toward the flow of beige-colored talk.

Mother was at the far side of the room. He noticed first her color and the contrast with everything else around her. She was in white, so it was not actual color he saw, but the sense of excitement in her face and in her voice. He heard her say she'd just come off duty at the hospital; then her dress was a uniform. Had she been a doctor, he could not have approached, but a nurse was approachable. He thought she was beautiful, though not beautiful like his fantasies. She was short, with a small waist and large breasts and hips, not the willowy woman of his dreams. With her brown skin, dark hair and eyes, and especially her mischievous look, she made him think of a gypsy, a gypsy with jokes and secrets she might or might not tell.

Mrs. Jessup came up beside him. "This is someone you should meet, Will. Bess March. She was born here. You could try out your Arabic on her."

He blessed Mrs. Jessup for smoothing the way and began to tell Miss March the Jehah story he had just learned from his tutor in Arabic: "Jehah, the wise fool, could never resist a bet. His friends bet him he couldn't last out a night on the snowy hillside without clothes or a fire, so he said he would do it. If he succeeded they would cook him a feast; if he failed he would cook them one. How he suffered. All that kept him going was the sight of a tiny candle in a window some miles away and he kept his eyes on that."

The thought went through Will's head that this was an absurd story and she probably knew it already, but she was looking at him as if to catch every word.

He struggled through to the end. "When Jehah told his

friends how his night had been and how only the light of the candle had given him comfort, they laughed and said, 'Ah, but Jehah, you cheated us with that candle. How can you expect us to reward you?' Jehah could hardly believe what was happening. Finally though, he smiled and said, 'Come my friends, I have been a fool as I am so often. Come to my house tomorrow and I will roast a whole lamb for us to eat.' The next day the friends came to Jehah's house early, talking and laughing while they waited. Finally they grew faint with hunger and said to Jehah, 'How is the lamb coming? When will we eat?' 'Soon, soon,' said Jehah and he led them to where the lamb hung, stuffed and trussed, over a small lighted candle. 'You see, my brothers, it will be ready soon.'"

Miss March said, *"Aaffek, ya shattir."* ("Good for you, clever one.") She smiled up at him.

By the end of the afternoon he could see that Miss March, Elizabeth (she hated "Bess"), fit neither of the two pigeonholes he had constructed for women: temptresses, who enticed men to acts of shame from which they never recovered, or pure women, like his mother. Sometimes in Chicago he used to glimpse some of that first kind, and then for many nights afterward would yearn for them. His dreams shocked him. Any good woman who learned about his secret yearnings would naturally want nothing further to do with him. That's what he'd always thought, but now that he'd met Elizabeth March he thought maybe his secrets would be safe with her. Not that she would approve or share them. He could tell she was a good woman.

Instead of walking back up to Souk that evening, he stayed in Beirut. She had said she was on night duty. He was waiting at the front entrance of the American University Hospital at seven the next morning when her shift would be over. Other night nurses came out and he thought each one would be Elizabeth. Just as he was giving up, she came out. Her nurse's cap rested like a small bird on top of her hair, in wisps after her hours on duty. She wore a navy blue cape over her uniform.

He was so glad to see her that he rushed up and told her

so, instead of pretending he was just passing by. She said he could walk with her to her parents' house in the American compound.

She was quieter now than at tea the day before, making him afraid he had offended her or that she didn't want to see him again so soon. No, she said, she was just tired. She was head nurse in the operating room and last night there'd been two long operations. She told him this matter-of-factly but with pride, and he listened, impressed by her knowledge and intrigued as always by any medical talk.

She invited him in to meet her parents. Like the Jessups, the Marches were early missionaries to Syria. Elizabeth had told him that her father often dressed as an Arab when he toured the interior on horseback. He enjoyed being mistaken for an Arab, she said, and besides it was safer that way. Will thought about what it would be like to be taken for an Arab, to have done important work here and to be revered for it.

Mother had told me a little about their courtship. He had no experience with a woman, no intimacy, not even friendship. He and his oldest sister had shared the chores and responsibility like two workhorses; his favorite sister was the quiet pretty one, but he hardly knew her. The other two sisters were so much younger, they always remained little girls to him. Growing up, he had avoided girls in school and later any women his own age, seeing them always as either too good or too bad. So now he was unsure of himself, though sure of what he wanted—to marry Elizabeth. As for her, she was reluctant to give up her nursing and her freedom, knowing her life would be ruled by Will if she were to marry him.

They went on a horseback trip with some other young couples to Mt. Herman and became officially engaged. I wonder when Father decided to propose and what he said, and if Mother felt reluctant still or if something happened to dispel her doubts. She did tell me she saw his goodness then, his seriousness, and his love of his mother. She'd noticed how courtly he was with her mother and with Mrs. Jessup. Most important of all, she thought he would be a good father.

As a child I had seen snapshots of the group standing beside their horses in the shadow of the Lebanon mountains. The women were wearing riding habits down to their ankles and hats with dust veils, the men wore pith helmets. They slept in two canvas tents, women decorously in one and men in the other.

What he saw in her on the camping trip was her playfulness, her ease and warmth with other people, and her fascinating medical knowledge. He felt happy around her.

They married in the American Church in Beirut, September 1914, he in his dark suit and high starched collar, Elizabeth in white, with a train and a veil with an orange blossom wreath. He was thirty, she was twenty-eight.

Dr. Jessup performed the service and the whole mission community was in attendance. Some of the wedding guests walked to the wedding barefoot, carrying their shoes, because already good shoes were in short supply. World War I was to break out a month later. Even more immediate was the massacre of Armenians by the Turks. There was great poverty; starvation and epidemics of typhus and cholera followed. But on this day no one thought about those things. The wedding couple hired the finest carriage, shiny black with bright yellow wheels and high-stepping black horses. They drove off to a *pension* in Brumana for their honeymoon.

Will was morally opposed to birth control and thought they should not consummate their marriage for a year. My mother didn't tell me whether this decision came as a surprise in Brumana or whether they'd talked about it during their engagement. Whichever way, she was relieved rather than disappointed to put off what she saw as an unpleasant necessity. She was aware of having limited time ahead to have the four children she wanted, but still she felt reprieved. She said she never did have any sexual feelings but came the closest to having them then. She was never again as happy with Will as that year when he was so attentive to her.

For my father that must have been a time of torment. He told Mother shame-facedly that he was oversexed, a cross he had to bear. How else to explain how he kept wanting to touch her, could hardly think of anything else. Since marriage hadn't cured him, but rather made him worse, he resigned himself to being oversexed for life, always on guard. That she was devoid of sexual feelings, as far as he could tell, confirmed that she was good like his mother, morally superior to him.

Later in their marriage Mother persuaded him to ease up on his commitment to abstinence, but the act was always hasty and surrounded by feelings of guilt and distress. On guard, he made himself avoid kissing or hugging. He seldom touched Mother in public or even in front of us, and when he kissed her he only kissed on the cheek.

The Mission sent them to Zahleh, where they set up house-keeping in an old stone manse. In winter cold wind whistled through it; in summer the sirocco wind suffocated them.

Father felt his real life as an adult had begun. He was through with his lessons in Arabic, a full member of the Presby-terian Mission assigned to the field, and married. There were a cook and a maid, and proper meals in a dining room with Eliza-beth sitting opposite him. There was a white linen cloth on the table and initialed napkin rings at the left of their plates.

Two years later in 1916, Elizabeth bore their first child, a son, at the University Hospital in Beirut. Will was shaken and so happy he wanted to name the baby Farrah, which means happi-ness in Arabic, but Elizabeth wouldn't agree to it. Their son was an American. He would have American playmates and go to an American school, so he needed an American name. They settled on Arthur. He was dark and small like Elizabeth's side of the family, high-strung and active.

In 1919 Will and Elizabeth's second son was born and named Philip. He was sturdy and contented, light of skin and hair, more like Will's side.

Will was a father who got up at night for crying babies, even though Elizabeth nursed them. He played with them, bathed them, changed their diapers as a matter of course, as few men of his era did. When he had to be away from home for several days, he considered it a hardship and got back as soon as he could.

I think in those early years Will saw Elizabeth as the ideal mother. She had given him two sons already, nursed them amply from the breasts he found so beautiful, knew exactly what was wrong from colic to cradle cap to croup, and could cure anything.

When Philip was just starting to walk he had an accident that demanded medical skill from Elizabeth and patience they didn't know they had from both of them. It happened when she was washing out some baby clothes with a teakettle of boiling water on the floor at her feet. Philip toddled over to be near her and companionably sat on the hot teakettle. He jumped off, but his diaper hooked the lid of the kettle and scalding water hit his upper leg and abdomen. For a while they didn't know if he would live. When the worst anxiety had passed, there began the long round-the-clock care of a small boy in terrible pain, as well as attention to Arthur, who angrily saw inordinate amounts of it going to his tiresome baby brother. The American Hospital and their family doctor were far away in Beirut, as were Elizabeth's parents. Will and Elizabeth turned to each other to get through the long ordeal of isolation and fear. I like to think of my parents then, close and feeling blessed when the crisis was past.

When Arthur was six, Mother started teaching him to read. She was an impatient, tense teacher, he an edgy little boy and her first pupil. He did learn to read finally and out of sheer determination even became a doctor, fulfilling his father's dream. But that first year, the frustrated tears they both shed made Elizabeth decide to postpone school for a while. Father bought two goats and the boys spent hours herding them through the dry, rocky fields. They looked like goatherds too—barefoot, very brown, wearing bright crocheted skullcaps.

Mother was pregnant again and hoped for a girl. The baby

was due April 1, 1922, but Grandmother March thought an April Fool baby should be avoided at all costs. As the time grew short, she urged Father to take Mother in a carriage over a particularly rocky stretch of road outside Beirut to hurry things along. And so I was satisfactorily born two days early. My parents, along with Grandma, were proud of what they had saved me from. My father was present for my birth, the only birth he attended.

Father wanted to name me Elizabeth, for Mother and his mother, or Frances, for his favorite sister, but Mother named me Margaret, for her favorite doll.

They were happy about having a girl. Father was affectionate and easy with me, roughhousing, as he did with my brothers, and carrying me high on his shoulders or piggy-back at the end of long walks around Zahleh. The family pictures of those years show only good times (families don't take pictures of their bad times, I suppose), but they are the times I remember too: family picnics, mud pies, doll tea parties, and my brothers herding the goats.

My only misery was naps. At three, after I refused to take them any longer in my white iron crib, I would take them if I could lie next to Father on the brass double bed. When he had to be away, I remember being furious and inconsolable that he would leave me. To comfort me, Mother used to place on my pillow near my head a small picture of him in a round mosaic frame.

My parents had their fourth child, a second girl, and considered their family complete. Anna, like Arthur, was small and dark, not plump and calm like Philip and me. She had amoebic dysentery almost from birth. Being chronically ill and the last chick made her special to Father. He began to refer to her as *Husti* ("my share").

As I grew older, around five or six, he stopped roughhousing with me and giving me piggyback rides. I became aware of a sort of seismic shift in my world with that loss. I wondered what had happened to cause him to change. I've come to think he could love me well when I was a small child, but when his anxiety got in the way he felt he had to back off to be safe.

At about the same time, my eyes and ears sharpened to take in new things I hadn't noticed when I was younger: how sometimes he would clamp his jaw and say nothing, would walk with heavy heels to his study and slam the door. This might be if Arthur or Philip didn't come right away when called or wouldn't say who hit the other first. He would do the same if Mother spent too much money or spent it on the wrong things. I noticed the redness at the back of his neck, the swelling vein at the side, and the iron in his measured words.

I saw that Mother didn't stand up to him, but wilted before a showdown. I was startled when I realized she was afraid of him, and decided to be her defender and champion. Besides, I could count on loving admiration and tolerance from her, whereas Father had a sermon for the slightest mistake and an air of waiting for the mistake to be made.

I hardened myself toward him. Seeing that he apparently didn't love me anymore, I forgot that he ever had. I assumed the attitude, *If you don't love me, then I won't love you.*

In 1927 the mission moved our family from the stone manse in Zahleh, from the yard with the mulberry trees and dry winds, to another stone house in Souk-el-Gharb, this one with *zinzilachts* in the yard. Now we were closer to Beirut, where we could board at the American Community School when we were old enough. One after the other we went.

Our leaving home gave Mother more time to care for the sick in the village. There were two midwives, so she didn't deliver babies, but she often visited young mothers with children at home, and the elderly. Father's work continued as before, examining schools and settling disputes between ministers and congregations.

Every month or so Father went to Beirut to consult with Fräulein Stokes, the matron, to see how each of us was doing. Her reports had few surprises: Arthur could be expected to cooperate and was studying and using his time productively;

Philip teased and was a daredevil and cutup. She found a letter he had written to a girl and passed it on to Father, causing a furor at home. I overheard bits of whispered conferences he and Mother had about how to deal with the matter. Father worried about Philip's character. Had Philip perhaps inherited the affliction of being oversexed? Mother thought Philip was just a normal curious adolescent. To be on the safe side, she agreed with Father to keep him at home for the last month of school before summer.

When I look back to those days I see Father's brown eyes. (I read a poem once by Maxine Kumin, "The Retrieval System," with the line, ". . . my dog, now dead, who all his long life carried about in his head the brown eyes of my father . . .") He had a firm, serious mouth and a full moustache, reddish and springy, later soft and gray. He was slim, always, and straight. Sometimes he wore a *tarboush* (fez) and would be taken for an Arab as my grandfather had been. He and his Syrian friends used to talk and laugh together, exchanging the Arab proverbs he liked to collect. He still loved Jehah stories and told them well. *"Ken ma ken ... "* the story would begin. ("It happened and it didn't happen....") Evening visits often included a time of storytelling. The others would coax Father to tell his latest Jehah story. A part of him would hold back, the consciousness that "life is real, life is earnest," as eight-year-old Willie had known, no time for idle chatter and laughing. At such moments he would stop, get serious and silent. The others would grow silent too.

"Let us pray," he would say, ending the levity for the evening. When I was growing up, I used to experience angry embarrassment over his "let us pray."

Whatever moral decision he came to, he acted on. Having decided it was wrong to do secular business or travel anywhere for secular purposes on Sunday, he followed his decision with an iron rule for us all. On Sundays, if we were home from boarding school, everyone walked to church, then home. There would be a family walk in the afternoon. The car might be used to go to a religious service, but nothing else, and even public transportation had to be avoided because conductors, bus drivers, and taxi drivers should not be asked to work on Sunday.

I remember when a Syrian friend of Father's invited us to a program at his new school on a Sunday afternoon. Father understood the program was to be a religious one, so he accepted and drove us to the school some miles away. The school director ushered us to seats of honor in the front and the program began: songs, skits, student speeches, but nothing religious. Father got fidgety, looked at the program sheet again, looked over to the director to question how this could be. His friend smiled. Father stood up and started herding us toward the car.

Mother said, "Will, I know how you feel, but we're here now. Shouldn't we just stay?"

He didn't bother with an answer but kept walking to the car.

The director rushed over to intercept him. "Dear friend," he said. "It means so much to me to have you see how my school is progressing. I know your opinion about Sunday, but we had to put the program on this day and I was afraid you wouldn't come. Please stay now that you are here. See, your children are enjoying this. Your wife wants to stay."

Little did he know my father. Nothing could have made him stay. Ever after that, when the friend's name came up, Father's expression would say, *He deceived me.*

Any picture of my father would be incomplete without his car and him as a driver. His first car was a Model T, a gift from his church in Springfield. He had never driven up to then and knew nothing about cars, so he hired a local man to be the family chauffeur and to give him lessons. He did learn to drive, but he was an erratic, impatient driver. Our family and friends learned to be quiet and hold on to the sides.

Once his car hit a child in a village street. I remember sitting in the back seat and live again the frozen moment before the child crawled out from under the car, screaming with fright, but not hurt. Another time Father was driving the family up the mountains to Zahleh late at night on the narrow winding road. He came up behind an ox-drawn wagon of hay, honked, then honked again at the driver, who continued plodding up the middle of the road. Impatient always when anything delayed him, Father now became thoroughly angry and tried to pass on the outside. As he did, the right front wheel of the wagon caught the left wheel of our car and pushed it off the side of the steep dirt embankment, where it hung at an angle, balanced on a bush. We inched out of the car. A crowd gathered in the dark from the village below to exclaim and look. Some of the men unhooked the car carefully and the oxen pulled it back onto the road. Arthur remembers that we sang the doxology when we got back in the car. "Praise God from whom all blessings flow."

Father wore an air of injured self-righteousness when we talked about those occurrences. The village child had run out carelessly in front of the car, so Father was not to blame for hitting him; the driver of the cart had tried Father's patience so long that he had to pass, even on the outside. Needing to be right was characteristic and so was his fierce defense of his rightness, as though it were his life.

I have come to realize that I behave in the same way when I am frightened or guilty. Then I act without regard to what might be the reasonable way. I discover that in myself, and then rediscover it, surprised each time at how my father lives in me. Hello, Father!

I don't remember being afraid he would die suddenly; I'm sure I thought he would live forever, but I can remember that he worried about his health, especially his heart. In college he had strained it running and described his heart as enlarged. When the summer baseball games started on Saturday afternoons, he batted but someone else ran for him. I remember him coming up to bat, getting into position, gripping his bat, hitting a good one, and then standing still looking after his runner. Did his legs twitch as he watched, as a dog's do when he dreams of chasing? Did he have a picture in his head of his too-large heart pumping away? Was he afraid?

Some time in the late '40s, I began to think about a visit to
Lebanon. I was homesick for its sights and smells and eager to
show it to my husband. True, our six-year-old son and two-year-
old daughter would be too young to remember anything they
saw, but they would travel well and probably enjoy it. My husband was a research associate at M.I.T., so our money was limited; but we had saved just enough to do it. Once we made the
decision I was very excited. Father and Mother were close to re-
tirement and it was important to me that we do this before they
left Lebanon for good. I wrote them of our plan, giving a tentative date of arrival.

After a few weeks my father wrote back. His letters were always typed, always formal and careful. This one started out telling about what was going on with his mission work, about the
weather, his health and Mother's. Then he wrote, "Your Mother
and I are pleased, of course, that you are contemplating a visit.
Let me say that it would be important that you put aside an
amount of money equal to what you'll be spending on the trip
to give to charity."

My mother's letter expressed joy that we would be coming.

And yet we didn't go. I found it impossible to bypass his
moral opinion, if not his actual decree. Here I was, an adult,
married, with two children. During the intervening furlough,
he had treated me respectfully as an adult; I had been able to
view him from an adult position and understand him better. In
all that time, he hadn't attempted to control me, nor did I feel
his dominance. But when I read his letter, it was as though I
were a little girl back in Lebanon again, where my powerful father determined what I could and couldn't do. Gone was my
adult self, even the fifteen-year-old self who had stood her
ground with him.

I cried for days, then I wrote back that we would not be
coming after all. My father made no comment. My mother's letter said she had begged Father not to write as he had. She
mourned that we would not come and said she had been afraid

that this would happen.

I still don't know why I gave in as I did, but I don't feel angry with him. His conscience rode him and he could only obey.

He retired a little before seventy and he and Mother left Lebanon. Philip asked them to come to Louisville, Kentucky, to live in the ground-floor duplex where he and his family lived, so they could be close by. They agreed to it and Mother enjoyed being close to family after all the years apart. But Father chafed at idleness. He felt relieved when he could work as a supply minister for a small black church.

He and Mother made visits to each of us, then didn't visit for some time. Philip wrote that Father seemed withdrawn, quiet, maybe even depressed. He complained of anginal pains. Still he was unwilling to rest much and kept up a round of chores. He insisted on sweeping the front sidewalk several times a day, Philip said. He put up an easel on the front porch with a blackboard on it, where he carefully wrote out Bible passages. He would erase the board and write new passages several times a day, so passersby could see them.

He told Mother and Philip that he was afraid his work as a missionary counted for nothing, that he had never really changed any lives. He was disappointed that none of his children had chosen to become missionaries and thought that pointed further to his failure. Only one of us, Philip, was even religious; the other three, markedly anti-religious. That seemed like a rejection of all that he stood for, a terrible disappointment. He sent Bibles to each of us, with a list of passages at the front that he said were to help in time of need.

My father died soon afterwards of a massive heart attack. He had woken up very early having difficulty breathing and called out to my mother. He died almost immediately.

Philip telephoned me where I was living with my husband and three young children in Concord, outside Boston, not an impossible distance away, but enough. If I were to go to Louisville, arrangements would have to be made for the children's care. We were always short of money and I thought of the plane fare. But even as I went through all those excuses, I knew they were only excuses. The real reason I didn't want to go to his funeral was that I couldn't summon up any grief for him. I no longer resented him. I could listen now to his opinions and not feel hemmed in, but I couldn't remember loving him. I seemed to feel no response at all to his dying. I didn't go.

Several years went by. My mother died and I went to her funeral. I wept for her, though still not for my father. Then one day I received a small package in the mail from Philip. The note with it said, "I was going over some of Father's things and found this. Thought you might want it."

It was an old cloth map, worn in the folds, and mottled brown in spots. I had to look closely to make out its faded colors and tiny drawings. I looked at the camels with curiosity, remembering how hard they'd been to do and how proud of them I'd been.

I remembered the place and the time when that project was begun. I was probably fourteen and we were all in the upstairs living room after supper. My father had his measuring tape and drawing materials laid out on a folding table by the stove. He was going to draw the map of Lebanon on cloth so it would be easy to carry and tack up in front when he gave his missionary talks on furlough. He showed me how he planned to do it, using crayons to blue in the rivers and the sea, brown for the mountains, dark green for the cedar groves.

I could still hear his voice: "What do you think, Margaret? Do you think you could draw in some of the historic sites and show where the important crops grow?" I remember it sounded too much like a school project, serious and boring, not like drawing people or made-up scenes. Somehow I started, first putting the Roman ruins at Baalbek, the wheat in the Bekaa Valley, the orange and date groves on the coast. I drew mosques and minarets, a crusader castle, and a herd of camels near some black Bedouin tents. I remember holding off the moment when I'd have to say, "I think it's done." I did a last-minute drawing of a Phoenician boat off the coast of Tyre.

It all came back to me—the joy of doing it and the strong sense that my father truly valued me then.

And then I realized he had kept it all that time, long beyond any usefulness it had as a map. He kept it because I made it. I know he did.

For the first time, my eyes filled with tears and I cried for him and for me.